Poetry and Heroism

Poetry and Heroism

An Encounter with Kierkegaard

RICHARD McCOMBS

CASCADE *Books* • Eugene, Oregon

POETRY AND HEROISM
An Encounter with Kierkegaard

Copyright © 2025 Richard McCombs. All rights reserved. Except for brief quotations in critical publications or reviews, no part of this book may be reproduced in any manner without prior written permission from the publisher. Write: Permissions, Wipf and Stock Publishers, 199 W. 8th Ave., Suite 3, Eugene, OR 97401.

Cascade Books
An Imprint of Wipf and Stock Publishers
199 W. 8th Ave., Suite 3
Eugene, OR 97401

www.wipfandstock.com

PAPERBACK ISBN: 979-8-3852-0869-2
HARDCOVER ISBN: 979-8-3852-0870-8
EBOOK ISBN: 979-8-3852-0871-5

Cataloguing-in-Publication data:

Names: McCombs, Richard, author.

Title: Poetry and heroism : an encounter with Kierkegaard / Richard McCombs.

Description: Eugene, OR: Cascade Books, 2025 | Includes bibliographical references.

Identifiers: ISBN 979-8-3852-0869-2 (paperback) | ISBN 979-8-3852-0870-8 (hardcover) | ISBN 979-8-3852-0871-5 (ebook)

Subjects: LCSH: Kierkegaard, Søren, 1813–1855 | Kierkegaard, Søren, 1813–1855—Religion | Kierkegaard, Søren, 1813–1855—Criticism and interpretation

Classification: B4377 M336 2025 (paperback) | B4377 M336 (ebook)

04/04/25

To James Cutsinger, 1953–2020, my mentor and friend, who was a model for me of Socratic pedagogy, who supported and encouraged me with great generosity, and who, despite thinking he knew much, graciously responded to my disagreements with him, and was the best listener I have ever met.

I would like to thank several people for assistance with this book. Anthony Eagan read much of it, and gave helpful suggestions. My son John and my wife Acacia also commented helpfully on parts of the manuscript. I am grateful also to Dr. Merold Westphal, whose excellent lectures on Kierkegaard at Fordham University in the fall of 1992 were both inspiring and enlightening.

Contents

Abbreviations	ix
Introduction	1
Chapter One: The Choice of Life	12
Chapter Two: An Esthetic Fantasy, Kierkegaard-Style	28
Chapter Three: The Apology of a Married Man	47
Chapter Four: The Poet and the Hero of Faith	61
Chapter Five: The Most Interesting Man Who Ever Lived	74
Chapter Six: Contemporaneity with Christ	91
Chapter Seven: Kierkegaard as Truth Witness and as Single Individual	103
Conclusion	113
Bibliography	117

Abbreviations

AUP   *Attack Upon "Christendom,"* trans. Walter Lowrie (Princeton: Princeton University Press, 1968).

CUP   *Concluding Unscientific Postscript to "Philosophical Fragments,"* trans. Howard V. Hong and Edna H. Hong (Princeton: Princeton University Press, 1992).

EO 1   *Either/Or: Part I*, trans. Howard V. Hong and Edna H. Hong (Princeton: Princeton University Press, 1987).

EO 2   *Either/Or: Part II*, trans. Howard V. Hong and Edna H. Hong (Princeton: Princeton University Press, 1987).

EUD   *Eighteen Upbuilding Discourses*, , trans. Howard V. Hong and Edna H. Hong (Princeton, NJ: Princeton University Press, 1990).

FSE   *For Self-Examination* and *Judge for Yourself!*, trans. Howard V. Hong and Edna H. Hong (Princeton: Princeton University Press, 1990).

FT   *Fear and Trembling* and *Repetition*, trans. Howard V. Hong and Edna H. Hong (Princeton: Princeton University Press, 1983).

JC   "Johannes Climacus or *de omnibus dubitandum est*." See PF.

JP   *Søren Kierkegaard's Journals and Papers*, 7 vols., ed. and trans. Howard V. Hong and Edna H. Hong, assisted by Gregor Malantschuk (Bloomington: Indiana University Press, vol. 1: 1967; vol. 2: 1970; vols. 3 and 4: 1975; vols. 5–7: 1978).

L   *The Lily of the Field and the Bird of the Air: Three Godly Discourses*, trans. Bruce H. Kirmmse (Princeton: Princeton University Press, 2016).

ABBREVIATIONS

PC   *Practice in Christianity*, trans. Howard V. Hong and Edna H. Hong (Princeton: Princeton University Press, 1991).

PF   *Philosophical Fragments* and *Johannes Climacus*, trans. Howard V. Hong and Edna H. Hong (Princeton: Princeton University Press, 1985).

PV   "*The Point of View for my Work as an Author*," "*The Single Individual*," *On My Work as an Author*, and "*Armed Neutrality*," trans. Howard V. Hong and Edna H. Hong (Princeton: Princeton University Press, 1998).

R   *Repetition.* See FT.

SLW   *Stages on Life's Way*, trans. Howard V. Hong and Edna H. Hong (Princeton: Princeton University Press, 1998).

SUD   *The Sickness Unto Death*, trans. Howard V. Hong and Edna H. Hong (Princeton: Princeton University Press, 1980).

TM   *The "Moment"* and *Late Writings*, trans. Howard V. Hong and Edna H. Hong (Princeton: Princeton University Press, 1998).

WA   *Without Authority*, trans. Howard V. Hong and Edna H. Hong (Princeton: Princeton University Press, 1997).

WL   *Works of Love*, trans. Howard V. Hong and Edna H. Hong (Princeton: Princeton University Press, 1995).

Introduction

THE PURPOSE OF THIS book is not primarily to get you up to speed on Kierkegaard's basic ideas as quickly and as painlessly as possible. Instead I want to give you a sense of what I love about his writings, and what you might love too. Much of what is admirable and potentially life-changing in Kierkegaard's writings can be summed up in the words "poetry and heroism." If you are demoralized or despairing, Kierkegaard uses poetry and heroism to encourage you and give you hope. If you are perplexed about what sort of life you should live, Kierkegaard guides you with poetry about heroic life-possibilities. If you have sadly concluded that modern life consists of ever improving means to increasingly trivial goals, Kierkegaard reveals opportunities for poetry and heroism that lie concealed in even the most dreary and pinched of modern circumstances. If you think that poetry is for effete esthetes who are privileged to enjoy excessive leisure, or that heroism is for fantasizers who have never grown up, Kierkegaard makes manifest how poetry and heroism are relevant for serious adults living ordinary lives. Kierkegaard shows how you can be the hero of your own life. He reveals how your existence can be a passionate quest filled with delightful adventures. He discloses how a modern life can be beautiful and profoundly meaningful. And since he does all this with poetry and heroism, we will be focusing on these two things in this introductory book. Along the way, of course, you can expect to learn something about Kierkegaard's most important ideas. But you will learn about them as things that inspire and guide life, not as ends in themselves.

What Kierkegaard means by poetry is not primarily a literary genre. Poems do, however, offer a clue to what he means. Consider the phenomenon of poetic diction. There are words that have a poetic aroma, because they are beautiful, elevated, or archaic. For example, *using* an ax is not very poetic, but *wielding* one is. *Digging* a hole is mundane, but *delving* for gold is poetic. It is not just diction that confers a poetic quality upon something. Metaphors, images, and combinations of words can do this too. There are also topics, ideas, and themes of stories that evoke poetic feelings: like Robin Hood, romantic love, or the quest for the holy grail. Instead of saying that love of God is important to him, Kierkegaard says that this love has for him a "primal lyrical validity." Instead of saying that we should bravely apply our ideals to life, Kierkegaard speaks of a "knight of faith" who "absolutely expresses the sublime in the pedestrian." And instead of saying that someone was consistent, Kierkegaard says that he "remained true to his love."

The purpose of poetic language and ideas is to tear us out of the habitual, insipid, or lethargic way of experiencing the world into which we often fall. Poetry reveals beauty, grandeur, and profound meaning in things, and therefore enchants us, or fills us with wonder or admiration. If you have poetic awareness of beauty, or of things of great worth, you admire them. If you have poetic awareness of grandeur, you feel awe. If you have poetic awareness of the fact that the world transcends your understanding, you are filled with wonder. If you poetically perceive a transfigured world of beauties and wonders, you are enchanted. Poetry aims to make us see the world, other people, and ourselves as marvels. Through our poetic capacity we experience things in a way that makes some people write poetry, renders others reverentially silent, and inspires still others to attempt something grand.

Falling in love, as opposed to lusting after a sexy body, is poetic. When people fall in love, they want to use poetry to praise their beloved, or their love for the beloved, as beautifully as they can. But the main connection between poetry and falling in love is not that lovers write poetry, or would like to, but that they experience the beloved in a poetic way, and that their love poetically illumines people and places who have a part in the story of their romance, or even the whole world.

Two modes of reading can also illustrate poetry. Sometimes we read page-turning thrillers for excitement. But once we have read a potboiler, we have little subsequent use for it. We do not wish to linger over it. We also sometimes read, not for the excitement of finding out what happens in a series of suspenseful episodes, but for the ambience, wonder, and beauty of a story and its world. This feeling for the atmosphere that we find enchantingly beautiful is a gift of poetry. It is a great boon to be enchanted by reading a book, and it is a still greater blessing to feel enchanted by people, nature, and the world.

INTRODUCTION

Another example of poetry can be found in the bittersweet feeling that we get from some stories. There are tales that make us sad, but the sorrow is also somehow a delight. We regret that something valuable has been lost. But we also feel joy, perhaps because the loss of the valuable thing makes us deeply aware that things of great worth exist, have existed, or can exist. Thus the loss of something of great worth can become a window through which we see grand and beautiful possibilities. Our joyful sadness over great losses, or unfulfilled wishes, is the tribute that we pay to the wonderful things that we cannot have now, a way of remaining faithful to what we love, and a fountain of youth when the sordidness of life threatens to make us jaded or cynical.

Let us consider two extremes on the spectrum of human desire. At one end of this spectrum is the desire to scratch an itch. The desire is perhaps the least poetic of human desires. At the other end of the spectrum is longing, or yearning, or pining for something deeply valuable or meaningful. Similarly, fear of being poked with a needle is quite unpoetic, but a feeling of awe for something grand and perilous is highly poetic. When we feel awe, our feeling for grandeur or sublimity predominates, and our fear of danger is secondary.

It will be useful to forestall some possible misunderstandings. I may have given you the misleading impression that poetry, or the poetic person, is uniformly serious or solemn. But that is not so. Kierkegaard himself is eminently poetic, but also playful, witty, humorous, and ironic. If you poetically perceive high and wonderful things, then you will also recognize it when you run up against things not worthy of great seriousness. When you encounter trivial things or matters of secondary importance, you may express the right relation to them by playing with them, or jesting about them, or by being ironic. Thus a poetic person or a poetic mentality can or should have an artful rhythm that alternates between play and seriousness, or between prose and poetry.

We tend to think of poetry as elitist or exclusive. It requires talent to write it, we say, and sophisticated taste to enjoy it. We think that poetry is not in our control. It requires inspiration to write, and when we read or listen to it, either we "get it" or we don't. Kierkegaard disagrees with all this. Poetry, he claims, is a universal human inheritance. Admittedly, not everyone can write beautiful poetry. But everyone can *live poetically*, and that is much more important than being a world-famous poem-writer.

But is it really possible for everyone to live poetically? Perhaps you suspect Kierkegaard is exaggerating. Perhaps you think you detect a penchant for paradox that makes him say nonsense in order to dazzle us. How can he back up his promise of a poetic life for everyone, when so many people are obviously trapped in prosy and dreary circumstances?

It is the purpose of this book to show how Kierkegaard keeps his promise about the possibility of a poetic life for anyone who wants it and strives for it. But for now, I can give some hints and suggestions as to how a genuinely poetic life is within the reach of all human beings. People are more likely to fall in love, and thereby to live poetically, if they practice restraint in their sexual desires and activities. Blessed are the pure in heart, for they shall fall in love. People are more able to lose themselves in ecstatic enchantment if they are not obsessed with themselves, or resentful of greatness in other people. If we can behold things without egotistical self-preoccupation, then they may reveal themselves so potently that we stand outside ourselves in blissful ecstasy. Blessed are the humble, for they can joyfully admire the grandeur and wonder of the world. Although poetic inspiration cannot be manufactured on demand, it is also not wholly outside of our control. People who work and wait for inspiration or enchantment are more likely to find it. The poet John Donne, who delivered eloquent homilies, was asked why he wrote them out beforehand, and did not rely extemporaneously on the inspiration of the Holy Ghost. He responded that he did in fact rely on inspiration, but that he believed in giving the Paraclete as much time as possible to inspire him. People who cultivate outer and inner silence are more receptive to profound impressions from things than chatterboxes whose minds are hotbeds of frenzied agitation. Similarly, people who preserve a youthful trust in things are more able to perceive the poetry of the world and of life than people who succumb to a cynical or nihilistic worldview. Again, people who are honest and unpretentious are more likely to discover their own voice and capacity for creativity, than people who are too eager to impress others, and therefore either strain too much for effect, or cheat by plagiaristic imitation of fashionable models. That is to say, people who seek their muse are more likely to find her than people who neglect to seek her, or flee her, or put up walls to keep her out. It normally requires hard work and sacrifice to write great poetry, or to make great poetry in one's life. For example, the most famous haiku poet, Basho, went on a long and dangerous journey to the north of Japan in search of inspiration and occasions for his art. In summary, there is much that we can do to cultivate both a sensitivity to the poetry of life and the capacity to live poetically.

Now that I have given you a rough idea of poetry, and defended the claim that "living poetically" is within the reach of everyone, let us consider what Kierkegaard himself specifically means by poetry. He conceives of it as something that *praises* or appreciates things of the greatest worth, which he calls *ideals*.[1] Foremost among the Christian ideals that he praises are faith, hope, and love. He also praises human ideals, such as the good, the true, and the beautiful (TM 225). Kierkegaard poetically praises ideals in order to inspire his readers to admire them, wonder at them, feel grateful for them, adore them, and more.

Obviously, poetic appreciation of ideals is delightful. It is a joy to contemplate things of great worth or of ideal beauty. But Kierkegaard does not write in order to recommend or excuse mere contemplation of ideals. That would be an esthetic indulgence. Instead, he writes to inspire people to serve and imitate the ideals in their lives. In other words, he praises models of perfection in order to invite people to live poetically, by expressing profound awareness of these models in their words, deeds, thoughts, feelings, gestures, and postures.

One of the most important parts of the poetry of life is heroism. Our poetic sensibility makes us admire heroic deeds, and inspires us to become heroes ourselves. Let us consider the nature of heroism. An important trait of heroes is that their tasks are difficult, and therefore require struggle. The poet Tennyson well captures the poetry of heroic struggle when he imagines an aged Odysseus who is weak in body, but "strong in will to strive, to seek, to find, and not to yield." Heroes strive, not for something trivial, but for something grand—a great spiritual, ethical, or political good. Often part of their struggle is to face formidable dangers, like death; and they may sacrifice their lives to their great purpose. Some heroes create something. Among these are the founders of states, or of religions, or of sciences. Some heroes preserve something. Among these are defenders or rulers of states in times of crisis, like Horatio at the bridge, or Winston Churchill in World War II. Some heroes aim to restore something, like the great figures of the Protestant Reformation or of the Renaissance. There are heroes of war, of the quest, of exploration, and of adventure. Most heroes have at least some of the following virtues: nobility, courage, resourcefulness, resoluteness,

---

1. For a fuller account of Kierkegaard's understanding and use of poetry as praise of heroes and ideals, see McCombs, *Art and Praise*, 1–7.

resilience, and perseverance. Because they reveal the sublime heights of human potential, heroes are, or deserve to be, admired, imitated, or followed, especially when their deeds are celebrated by a worthy poet.

Supposing we grant that heroism is exciting and admirable, what then does that have to do with you and me? Even in heroic ages of the world, few people could become heroes; and in the world of today there are fewer opportunities for heroism than ever before. As latecomers in history, we are dwarfed by the accomplishments of the past. So much has already been done that it seems there are few great deeds left for an aspiring hero to do. We are small beings caught in the gigantic social, political, and economic webs of modern life, so that we have little power to influence the course of events. In former times members of small tribes had numerous opportunities to perform a significant service for their people. But it is discouragingly difficult to stand out as a benefactor of a large modern state. There is also the fact that the overarching tendency of Western civilization is towards equality, and this tendency drastically diminishes heroic possibilities. In short, heroism now seems out of date, increasingly less possible, and therefore more or less irrelevant.

The worst of heroism, however, is not its irrelevance. Heroism also seems to be irrational, unhealthy, and sometimes catastrophically destructive. Perhaps we are better off saying good riddance to heroes with their perils. For they often pick fights or provoke wars. They tend to be excessively competitive, and insufficiently cooperative. When they have their way, there can be too much conflict, and not enough collaboration and compromise. Heroes tend to be immoderate, extreme, or excessively ambitious. They often try to achieve too much, and thus lose, or make us lose, what we have, or make us fail to achieve what we realistically could have accomplished. Countless people have perished as collateral damage in the fall of a hero who insanely pursued an impossible dream. Sacrifice is a heroic word, and sometimes sacrifices are necessary. But heroes are too prone to sacrifice themselves and others, even when there is no pressing need for this. Many heroes love their own glory more than the things that they profess to serve, with the result that they destroy the common good in pursuit of their individual fame. Many would-be heroes have guided or goaded their countries into unnecessary and risky wars in order to have a chance at winning immortal fame for themselves, when the wiser course would have been to stay quietly at home. Many glory-seeking heroes have gotten their troops killed when the risk was ill-advised. Many would-be heroes

Introduction

have ruined a thriving enterprise because they wanted to put their personal stamp on it. A large part of the good that a hero should do for others is to be a model of excellence. But heroes are often faulty exemplars, because they tend to overvalue martial virtues, like courage, audacity, strength, and unyielding resolution, and to undervalue other, perhaps greater, goods and virtues, like wisdom, peace, and political stability. Similarly, they may desire too much to earn their pleasures, and not know how to enjoy a gift, or leisure. They are therefore dangerous models if we want to live in a healthy and reasonable manner. Because wisdom is not the strong point of many heroes, they are often easy to manipulate and exploit. They can be tricked into serving an unworthy cause, or even a wicked one. Clever opportunists can use heroes as figureheads for their harmful or selfish projects. We are suckers for heroes, so that a con man with a hero as a poster boy has a good chance of making fools of us. Perhaps the worst thing of all about heroes is that they tend to have excessively large egos, and we all know from experience many problems that egoism can cause. To be as negative as possible, we might say that heroism is the glorification, or even the apotheosis, of pernicious pride.

It can be great fun to criticize heroism as something dangerous and unreasonable, whether we are motivated by wisdom, or perhaps by cowardice or envy; and I went on for a long time indulging myself in berating the evils of heroism. But such criticism cannot quash the roots of heroism in human nature. We have a deep and hard to eradicate desire to be heroic. Nearly all religions testify to the power of egoism and to the difficulty of combating it, as do many nonreligious thinkers. Jean Paul Sartre argues that "man fundamentally is the desire to be God."[2] Jean-Jacques Rousseau argues that a "universal desire for reputation, honors, and privileges . . . devours us all."[3] Similarly our own experience, and many prominent features of human life, witness to the strength and all-pervasiveness of the desire for heroism. All or nearly all people at least sometimes indulge in ego-flattering daydreams or fantasies of heroic success. Many people vicariously enjoy the heroics of fictional characters in novels or films. Sports fans vicariously glory in the heroic success of their favorite players or teams. Games are a ubiquitous part of human life, and most games are imitations of heroic activities, like wars, quests, or adventures. We often play games in order

---

2. Sartre, *Existentialism and Human Emotions*, 63.

3. Rousseau, *Discourse on the Origin and Foundations of Inequality*, in *Basic Political Writings*, 88.

to inject what might be called safe and easy heroism into our lives. It is striking to what degree sex has been celebrated as heroic. For in connection with it we speak of prowess, potency, conquests, exploits, adventures, rivals, and a trophy wife; and many people boast about their sexual exploits as if they were heroic deeds. Moneymaking is also talked about in heroic terms. For example, we speak of competition in the market, and of venture capitalism; and people deeply admire the titans of finance.

Many of our ideals and standards of success are heroic, or crypto-heroic. Most of us would say that we want to be individuals, perhaps even "rugged individualists." To be an individual is to be self-reliant, or to stand alone, or to be courageous enough to think for oneself and to act resolutely on one's independent judgment, despite great pressure to conform to the herd. In short, to be an individual is to be strong and courageous enough to resist forces outside oneself that threaten to control one's thoughts and deeds. Our conception of maturity, or adulthood, is similarly heroic. We think an adult is independent, which I have already argued is quite difficult, as have many philosophers, existentialists, and religious thinkers. We believe that becoming truly mature means fulfilling one's potential. But this is no easy matter, and most of us do not come close to fulfilling it. We say that becoming an adult means being capable of meeting life's challenges with resourcefulness and dignity. But given how formidable life's challenges can be, adequate readiness for them is a heroic task, and therefore requires rigorous training. In short, it almost seems that our idea of adulthood is virtually the same as our idea of heroism. It is often said that really to live means to pursue one's dreams, or not to settle or compromise. But if we are honest with ourselves, we must admit that we want quite a lot out of life, so that following our dreams would be a heroic endeavor.

Many great psychologists explain that there is much mental illness that results either from a lack of heroic qualities like courage and resilience, or from a frustrated desire to be heroic. Carl Jung writes that the "disinclination to face stern reality is the distinguishing feature of . . . fantasies" of neurotics.[4] Alfred Adler claims that the neurotic person "is constantly trying to furnish proof for his superiority," and has an "enormously powerful need for a feeling of self-worth."[5] Interpreting Freud, Norman Brown

---

4. Jung, *Jung Contra Freud*, 48.
5. Adler, *Neurotic Character*, xviii.

INTRODUCTION

writes that the "infantile conflict between actual impotence and dreams of omnipotence is . . . the basic theme of the universal history of mankind."[6]

If the desire for heroism is ineradicable, but often pathological in its consequences, the question arises of what to do about this problematic part of human nature. Perhaps we should try to moderate it, or to direct it into healthy channels, or to limit the damage that it does. But whatever our proposed solution may be, it will certainly not be easy to put it into practice. There are some thinkers who argue that the remedy to this problem is to see how ordinary life affords ample opportunities for sane and healthy heroics. Consider these quotations from the sensible Montaigne: "Any man who could bear with valor the mischances of ordinary life would have no need to be more courageous on becoming a soldier"; "If you have been able to examine and manage your own life you have achieved the greatest task of all"; and "Our most great and glorious achievement is to live our life fittingly."[7] In short, Montaigne tells us that ordinary life affords sufficient opportunities for heroism, so that there is no need either to feel dissatisfied with everyday reality, or to seek out extreme situations. Similarly, Samuel Johnson extols inconspicuous heroism: "But he has no reason to repine though his abilities are small and his opportunities few. He that has improved the virtue or advanced the happiness of one fellow-creature, he that has ascertained a single moral proposition, or added one useful experiment to natural knowledge, may be contented with his own performance, and, with respect to mortals like himself, may demand, like *Augustus*, to be dismissed at his departure with applause."[8] According to Johnson, not only does ordinary life afford adequate opportunities for heroism, but many people actually take advantage of them, and should be proud of doing so, instead of feeling frustrated owing to their lack of world-historical fame.

Many religions vehemently chasten, and enthusiastically encourage, the heroic impulse. They infinitely chasten it by demanding that one must slay the dragon of pride. They infinitely encourage it by demanding that one imitate God. Kierkegaard thinks that Christianity requires heroism of all people, writing that "Christian heroism" is "to venture wholly to become oneself, an individual human being, this specific individual human being, alone before God, alone in this prodigious strenuousness and this prodigious responsibility" (SUD 5). But, since there is the ever-present danger

6. Brown, *Life Against Death*, 25.
7. Montaigne, "On Experience," 402, 415–16.
8. Johnson, *Selected Essays*, No. 88, 484.

of vicious pride, Kierkegaard thinks that our heroic aspirations have to be tempered by extraordinary humility. Hence the hero of faith has "paradoxical and humble courage" (FT 49).

But, you may object, the combination of religion and heroism is fatal. Religion dangerously sanctions heroism by regarding God as its backer, and uses the idea of service to God to justify all sorts of atrocities. This is not the place to debate the question of the harmfulness or helpfulness of religion in history. To be sure, religion has either inspired, or been used to justify, many wrongs. But human beings have done great wrongs to one another without the aid of religion, and done great good in the world owing to their religion. It is also well to keep in mind that Christianity puts the highest value on humility and love, so that one cannot reasonably use it as an excuse for violence or oppression.

Kierkegaard deeply ponders the question to what extent a heroic Christian may risk doing harm to other people in his essay, "Does a Human Being Have the Right to Let Himself Be Put to Death for the Truth?" (WA 51). This essay makes "the assumption that with regard to courage everything is in due order and correct," and proceeds to inquire whether the courageous person has "the right for the sake of the truth to allow others to become guilty of a murder . . . *does not my duty to my fellow human beings* rather bid me to yield a little? How far does my duty to the truth reach, and how far my duty toward others?" (WA 68). Kierkegaard answers that only in exceptional circumstances does a person have the right to be martyred for one's faith: "only in the relation between Christianity and non-Christianity can being put to death for the truth take place in truth," because only then is a "person so situated that he dares truthfully to claim to have the absolute truth." "But in the relation between Christian and [merely nominal, or lukewarm] Christian," the right in question does not exist (WA 86). Thus Kierkegaard argues that in many cases a heroic Christian should not provoke or tempt people to kill him or her, thereby harming their own souls worse than his body. Admittedly Kierkegaard is often extreme, and his extremism is deeply rooted in his ideas about Christian heroism. But, as his essay on martyrdom shows, he is also lovingly concerned for his fellow human beings, and thinks carefully about how to use Christian heroism, not to harm, but to benefit, other people.

Let us summarize. Although heroism is dangerous, prone to excess, and often irrational, it is hard if not impossible to eradicate the desire for it. We naturally desire to be the heroes of our own lives. We need heroism to meet life's challenges and to pursue our ideals. Opportunities for heroism are ubiquitous in every life. And heroism is an important part of the poetry of life. Therefore we should think carefully about how to become heroic, and I invite you to take Kierkegaard as a guide in this inquiry.

It is no secret that Kierkegaard awards the prize for the most poetic and heroic life to Christianity, and we will accordingly explore his ideas about Christian poetry and heroism, and try to see why he judges that the knighthood of faith is greater than all other kinds of knighthood. But we should also do justice to the fact that Kierkegaard writes about a variety of poetic and heroic lives in a way that inspires many readers, including non-Christians. Part of his greatness as a poetic thinker is that he generously describes exciting and meaningful possibilities for many sorts of readers. As he puts it: "life has tasks enough also for the person who does not come to faith, and if he loves them honestly, his life will not be wasted, even if it is never comparable to the lives of those who perceived and grasped the highest" (FT 122). Hence we will investigate Kierkegaard's poetic presentation of a wide spectrum of heroic possibilities.

CHAPTER ONE

The Choice of Life

HUMAN LIFE POSES DIFFICULT and momentous questions. What kind of career should I pursue? Should I marry? How should I raise my children? Perhaps the most difficult and the most important question is how I should live. What is the best life for human beings in general, and for me in particular given my talents, temperament, and circumstances? Is the best life lived for myself, or for other people, or for a cause, or for an ideal, or for God? Alternatively, what counts as success in life? Is it wise to seek pleasure more than anything, or meaning, or the service of something greater than ourselves, or love, or fulfillment of our best capacities—and if so, what are those best capacities? And if we succeed in determining the best goal for our lives, what then are the means to achieving it?

Given the momentousness and difficulty of the choice of life, a second question arises: what is the best method of investigating how to live. There are many possible ways of seeking an answer. We could look to science for guidance, or to religion. We could personally experiment by trying out various ways of life, or observe, question, and ponder the lives of the people whom we encounter. We could study exemplary lives recorded in biographies. Or we might seek advice from a friend whom we admire and trust. Or perhaps we would prefer to consult self-help books. Or we might think that sound common sense is the best guide. Or, as is likely for most of us, we might combine two or more of these methods.

Plausible objections might be raised to any strategy for choosing a life, since every strategy has its peculiar strengths and weaknesses. Common sense is perhaps unlikely to lead to a disastrous choice of life. But it is also unlikely to lead to the best choice. It is much more probable that it would lead to a middling sort of existence. Moreover, there is the problem with common sense that it is not the same everywhere, but varies from place to place; and no particular version of it has the resources to prove, without begging the question, its superiority to its rivals. If instead we seek advice from someone we consider wise, perhaps there is a good chance that our advisor will provide us with a better answer than we could find for ourselves. But how do we determine who is the best advisor? By accepting the advice of one person we may be missing out on better advice from a more sage counselor. Much can be learned by reading biographies. But how do we decide which exemplary person, or which exemplary life, to imitate? Or, if we do not settle on just one model, how do we combine many models to make one coherent and excellent life-plan for ourselves? Certainly a prudent person makes use of his or her own experience in deciding how to live, and you can expand the range of your experiences by deliberately experimenting with different approaches to life. But difficulties lurk here too. Some experiments are dangerous and can cause harm from which it is difficult or impossible to recover. And some experiments take a long time to execute, because they require the acquisition of knowledge, skills, or habits of feeling. Often we do not know how enjoyable or fulfilling an activity or a way of life can be for us until after we have worked at it for months or years. Therefore the experimental approach can test only a limited number of options, and must leave untested many more kinds of life than it can responsibly evaluate. We can study many more kinds of lives in the people we meet than we can personally test, and careful study of people we encounter can teach us much. But it is hard to pass judgment on a way of life on the basis of a finite number of examples. Perhaps the people we observe living a given kind of life are not adequate examples of it. Perhaps they are not going about their ways of life optimally. Religion or faith has doubtlessly helped many people to lead good lives. But according to St. Peter, one needs to be ready to *give* a *reason* for one's religious *hope*.[1] How then does one explain to oneself or to other people one's hope and faith when one is aware that there are rival religions? Science is very good at seeking answers to some kinds of questions. But it is not designed to tell us whether we have any duties, and if so, what they are. Nor is it by nature equipped to assess the worth of things, or the criteria by which to assess worth. What experiments or scientific reasoning could tell us whether it is

---

1. 1 Pet 3:15. All translations of the New Testament are the author's.

wiser to seek physical pleasure, or meaning, or service to something higher, etc.? Self-help books are mostly popularizations of one or more of the above approaches to the question of how to live, so that they will have the same limitations as the things that they popularize, plus further limits that result from the superficiality of popularization. Combining two or more of the above approaches seems like a good idea, and many of us do this. But how to do it well? How to avoid working at cross-purposes with oneself when one combines approaches that may not be wholly compatible? How to cull the wheat and reject the chaff from life-plans formulated in many cases by people wiser than ourselves?

Although the choice of life is formidably difficult, you cannot avoid choosing, even for a little while. Your actual way of life implies an answer to the question of how to live, whether you are able to state or defend your answer or not. Given this undeniable fact, it seems prudent to take great care in formulating your life-plan. This is the almost impossible but nonetheless unavoidable task assigned to every human being. We can be extremely skeptical about the possibility of answering theoretical questions. But the practical question of how to live urgently demands an answer almost at every moment, and we give an answer willy-nilly in our actual way of life.

There are still other approaches to the problem of how to live. Socrates, in the *Republic*, refers to the "ancient quarrel between poetry and philosophy,"[2] and a principal part of this quarrel concerns the question of the best life. Let us briefly examine the two quarreling life-guides mentioned by Socrates, especially their strengths and weaknesses.

Once we pose the question of the wisest approach to the choice of life, and try to assess the strengths and weaknesses of various competing approaches, we are well on our way to doing philosophy. Philosophy uses reason to seek knowledge or wisdom, or at least reasonable opinions. It defines things, seeks to be consistent in its beliefs, argues for its opinions, raises objections to ideas, replies to objections, and refutes opinions that cannot stand up to scrutiny. It seeks to trace beliefs and belief systems back to their fundamental premises. It considers basic questions, like what is the best life, or what is the nature of human beings, of justice, or even of being. It also investigates questions of great generality that no special science considers, like what is knowledge, or what is a thing. These questions are very difficult, and philosophy has not answered them so definitively that people generally regarded as rational can all agree on the answers.

---

2. Plato, *Republic*, 607b. All translations of Plato are the author's.

Of course many of the things that philosophers do, other people do too, without calling themselves philosophers. Thus something like philosophy is almost unavoidable for human beings. Official philosophy tries to do better what most or all people do sometimes, when they are feeling especially thoughtful, or when they become troubled by the fact that they disagree with reasonable people about important basic questions, and then try to do something responsible about this disagreement.

Philosophy is beset with many difficulties, and philosophers are prone to certain mistakes or excesses. Most of the questions that philosophers ask are difficult to answer definitively, if not impossible. Philosophers tend to be too abstract, or prematurely general, or not sufficiently in touch with the particulars of experience. They may give too much weight to abstract reasoning, and not enough to imagination, feeling, experience, or empirical evidence. When they ask a practical question that demands an answer, they may get lost in thinking, and neglect to arrive at a decision, or delay the decision for too long, like Hamlet. It would be ridiculous to spend all one's life trying to answer the question of how to live, and not at some point put into practice one's best provisional answer to this question, unless the best life absurdly consists in investigating the question of the best life. Philosophers often become very skeptical. They begin by ambitiously seeking knowledge, but may end up deciding that they do or can know little or nothing, and then delight in showing other people that they do not know anything solid and important either. One of the greatest problems in philosophy concerns first principles. Philosophy makes logical arguments, and logical arguments require premises. Therefore we cannot use logic to establish all of our premises without arguing in a circle, which seems to be an irrational way of proceeding. It appears, then, that philosophy needs a way of knowing first principles that does not consist in arguing for them, or in mere faith, or in begging the question. This is a great difficulty.

By poetry Socrates does not mean beautiful, metrical language, but something like literature. Poetry often tells stories. It tends to seek beauty, drama, or interesting possibilities, more than it seeks truth. It uses and appeals more to imagination and feeling than to reason. It rarely engages in long and careful logical investigation. It seldom seeks to prove or refute ideas by rational argumentation. Poets tend to be more concerned with making something new than with knowing what is already real, and then acting in the world on the basis of this knowledge.

Thus it is obvious that poetry as defined by Socrates has many traits to which a philosopher would object. Since poets are not primarily logical investigators, they may lapse into confusion or inconsistency. Their use of imagination may lure them into fantasy and illusion. Their delight and indulgence in emotions may distort their judgment. They may say things because they are beautiful, or interesting, or dramatic, and not because they seem true upon sober examination. The kinds of fictional characters that they create so as to please and captivate an audience may not be good models to imitate in life; but since human beings are natural imitators, they may voluntarily or involuntarily imitate fictional characters to their detriment. In general poetry seems to encourage people to rely too much on their imagination and feelings, and to inflame these faculties into excessive activity, and to lull the rational faculty to sleep.

Despite its liabilities, poetry can be very useful in philosophical inquiry, and can even do things for philosophy that philosophy, narrowly defined, cannot do for itself. We should recall that Plato's writings are at least as poetic as they are philosophical. Poetic imagination can help a person get a glimpse of what it is like to be another person. A first-level accomplishment of this sort is to imagine being in the situation of another person. This person is faced with a dilemma. How would I feel, think, and act if I too were faced with that thorny problem? A second-level accomplishment, which is more difficult and more revealing, is to imagine what it is like to think, feel, and act as another person. This second level of imagination is the basis for a much better test of a way of life than merely imagining oneself, with one's own sensibility, in the place of someone else. If I want to know what it is like to live as a scientist, but lack both the habit of study and skill in experimentation, it is not enough for me to imagine myself, as I am now, devoted to scientific pursuits. Instead I must imagine myself transformed by work into a person eminently suited to a life in quest of scientific truth. Similarly, if a person who is cynical about patriotism tries to evaluate a patriotic life, it is not an adequate test for him to imagine himself, as he now is, behaving patriotically, but he must find a way to imagine thinking, feeling, and acting like a passionate patriot. Rousseau claims that the pleasures of an ardent patriot are one hundred times greater than those of any romantic lover.[3] If he is right, then the non-patriotic evaluator of patriotic life has a difficult task in attempting to approximate the inner experience of an enthusiastic lover of the homeland.

---

3. Rousseau, *Discourse on Political Economy*, , in *Basic Political Writings*, 134.

Philosophers often object to imagination because of its great power to distort our perception of reality, thus creating fantasies and illusions, and to deform the passions. But if imagination has such power for ill and error, it may also have great power for good and truth, as many drugs are both deadly poisons and potent medicines, depending on how they are used. Given that imagination can pervert the passions, rendering them contrary to reason, it seems likely that it could also be used to educate the passions, put them in line with reason, and help them to assist or cooperate with reason. Similarly, given imagination's capacity to direct the mind to errors and impossibilities, it seems likely that it also has the capacity to direct our minds to promising possibilities, so that we can become aware of them and explore them. Thus there are many ways that a philosopher could or should use imagination.

Socrates plausibly defines thinking as the soul's dialogue with itself.[4] This is to say that thinking means imagining an intelligent companion in conversation with yourself, who thinks differently from you, raises objections to your pet theories, comes at things from a different point of view from you, demands proof of your first impressions, and almost surprises you as it were with unexpected suggestions. A prosaic philosopher does not surprise himself with his own thoughts, because he is too disciplined, too cautious and restrained, and too impressed with his own reasoning. But a poetic or imaginative philosopher can surprise himself, by guessing how another person might respond to his or her ideas. In summary, thinking is the dramatic story of a dialogue that the soul creates for itself in order to seek understanding. Thus the best philosophical thinking is also poetic thinking.

Philosophers often describe philosophical reason as impersonal. It seeks to transcend the limitations of individuality, in order to know what all people would know if they also transcended themselves and became pure minds. We have a hint that poetic imagination is also a kind of self-transcendence, without being a transcendence of personhood. Poetic inquiry is, or can be, a transcendence of one's own peculiar personhood, in order to think and feel as if one were someone else. It is self-transcendence because it is self-othering; it is effective impersonation of another person. And this kind of self-transcendence is exactly the kind that is needed when the question is what kind of life to live, and when one is to live, not as an impersonal thinker unfortunately weighed down by the dross of personality,

---

4. Plato, *Theaetetus*, 189e.

but as a complete and integrated person. If one lives personally, then one must think personally, though not merely in one's idiosyncratic mode.

There is also a more general form of poetic or imaginative self-transcendence. Prosaic persons live under the tyranny of the actual. Reality, however, consists not just of actual things, but of possibilities. Genuine possibilities are real, because they really can become actual, or because there is a basis for them in reality. People are not always as trapped by circumstances as they think they are. There are usually alternatives, some of them better than current actualities. There may be a remedy to one's problem. We need an imaginative vision of possibility in order to escape the tyranny of the actual, and in order to dream up better ways to act or live. Imagination is a visionary who glimpses a new life, and the outline of a path to it.

Given the limitations both of poetry and of unpoetic philosophy, and their capacity to correct and complement one another, it makes sense to combine the methods of each of these in one's investigation of the choice of life. This is what Kierkegaard does, calling himself a "poet and a thinker" (WA 165). Although he does not call himself a philosopher, what he means by thinking (or *dialectic*) is close enough to philosophy for us not to worry about any differences between them in this introductory book. In the remainder of this chapter we will consider some important aspects of Kierkegaard's conception and use of poetry as part of thinking or as an aid to thinking.

Kierkegaard describes himself as a "poet who influences by means of the ideals" (FSE 21). The ideals that he speaks of are ideals of human personhood and human life. Appropriately, Kierkegaard most often talks about ideals by way of historical or imaginary human beings who represent them, and by way of stories about these representative human beings. For the best way of investigating and presenting an ideal of personhood must include a consideration of a person. Similarly, the best treatment of an ideal of human life must involve a story about a life lived for that ideal. An unpoetic philosopher would talk mostly about the ideas that are at the ground of the kinds of persons and lives that he or she wished to examine. However, a poetic dialectician, or dialectical poet such as Kierkegaard, does not talk merely about the ideas, but also about persons who live by these ideas, and the stories that these ideas lead to in their lives.

Ideal or representative persons might aptly be called heroes. By heroes I mean pure types, people who consistently live in a way that is grounded in their basic idea of life. Such persons are committed, uncompromising, and perhaps extreme, and it is therefore fitting to call them heroes. We might also denominate then heroes on the basis of the fact that they are exemplary. For one of the functions of heroes is to illustrate and exemplify a way of life. For example, nations use their heroes as admirable models of patriotic citizenship. Similarly, religions use the lives of saints to show their adherents inspiring examples of religious devotion and virtue. But, I should be clear, not all of the persons whom Kierkegaard uses to symbolize ways of life are wholly or even mostly admirable. Some of them are villains or scoundrels, and others are even demonic. But all of them are pure types, as consistent as it is possible for them to be in representing their respective ways of life with their respective advantages and disadvantages.

It is important to stress that Kierkegaard's idealized persons are more consistent than actual people usually are. You might suspect that this idealized consistency is a defect in Kierkegaard's writings. How can we arrive at truth by way of unrealistic images of people? The answer is that Kierkegaard does not write in order to show us a realistic picture of life as it is, but to show us life as it might be, to show us ideals to be abhorred and rejected, or to be admired and pursued. The question when encountering a Kierkegaardian hero is not, are real people exactly like him or her, but instead: do I admire this hero, and do I want to imitate him or her, or do I think I have a duty to imitate him or her, even if I cannot perfectly exemplify in my life the ideal that the hero poetically represents.

Many of Kierkegaard's heroes or villains are pseudonymous personae who, according to Kierkegaard's poetic fiction, write his books. This is to say that they are fictional first-person voices that speak as if they were the authors of Kierkegaard's texts. As Huckleberry Finn is the fictional author of a novel by Mark Twain, so Kierkegaard's pseudonyms are the imaginary authors or editors or contributors to books written by Kierkegaard. Kierkegaard has more than one reason for writing many of his books pseudonymously. The one that concerns us here is that he wishes to show his readers "poeticized personalities who say I," or to show us examples of people who are persons in a deep sense (JP 1 656). People who say I have profundity of personhood in several ways. They try to know themselves. They reflect on themselves in an attempt to take possession of themselves and not be possessed by the ideas or the influence of other people. Thus they take responsibility for what kind of people they are. They attempt to shape themselves and their lives according to their best lights. They do not rely on human authority, but make choices for themselves. They are mature.

They also have a rich inner life. Kierkegaard sometimes calls this interiority *subjectivity*. His heroes are subjective because they strive to be the self-aware subjects, responsible agents of their own thoughts and actions, and passionate strivers for ideals.

Kierkegaard's first-person heroes speak at length for themselves and their lives, thereby revealing a way of life from the inside. They show or hint at what it is like to be a certain kind of person living a certain kind of life. In reading their words we should attempt to sympathize with them, to feel and think with them, to imitate the movements of their minds and hearts. It is pleasant to do this, because they are enthusiastic and exciting. Kierkegaard makes them passionate and intense so that they may show us the best and purest version of a possible way of life. Much of Kierkegaard's greatness lies in his success in creating pseudonyms who communicate to readers their zeal for their ways of life. Having read them, we then have the task of trying to evaluate them and their ways of being in the world. Kierkegaard sometimes helps us to do this, usually by means of another pseudonym who comments on them or criticizes them.

Pseudonyms have an important but limited role in Kierkegaard's authorship. It is almost entirely true to say that Kierkegaard does not use pseudonyms in order to represent what he regards as the highest kinds of life. The greatest heroes in Kierkegaard's writings do not speak at length about themselves and their own lives. The reason for this is Kierkegaard's modesty. He does not presume to speak for perfection as if he himself were perfect. He might even think he does not know with sufficient accuracy what it is like from the inside to be a perfect example of the highest life. Therefore he adopts other means of pointing to the highest. One way that he directs his readers' attention to the ideal is through pseudonyms who admire the best types of heroes. Although these pseudonyms are not as great as the heroes whom they admire, they are still exemplary—exemplary admirers. They show us how to relate fittingly to greatness. It is utterly essential that we intensely admire heroes if there is to be any question of our taking the next step of imitating them. Without intense admiration of the hero there can be no serious attempt to become a replica of him or her. A large part of what Kierkegaard means when he calls himself a poet is that he expresses admiration for heroes, or that he praises heroes, in order to invite, challenge, or summon his readers to imitate them. The poet and the hero make a team. The hero is an example of what we might, or should, become;

and the poet describes and praises the hero so that we can appreciate the hero's worth and be attracted to the possibility of imitating him or her.

Let us consider Kierkegaard's use of pseudonyms to praise heroes. There is a great advantage to using a mere admirer to praise the highest. If the greatest hero were to praise the greatest heroism, he would be praising himself; and we do not like it when people praise themselves. Nor do we listen receptively to their self-praise. We are unlikely to catch fire and admire them as they admire themselves. An admirer who is not the ideal, but who praises it, is a much more effective eulogist of it than the ideal is of itself. This effective encomiast is precisely the poet. Kierkegaard carefully constructs his pseudonymous poets so that they can eulogize the hero as effectively as possible. Of course he makes them eloquent, as he himself is eloquent. And he makes them have a fairly good understanding of what they praise. He also creates them so that they have made significant progress in becoming like the hero, but not so like the hero that there is any danger of suspecting them of self-praise when they praise the hero. The poet needs to be somewhat like the hero in order to be qualified to praise him or her, but unlike the hero to avoid praising himself. How could the poet guess at what the hero is like unless the poet is somewhat like the hero? How could we listen receptively to the poet if he were praising himself? Thus the hero should be, in his personal development, in his progress along life's way, somewhere in between the average reader and the hero, in order to make a bridge between the *mediocre* and the perfect. Kierkegaard's term for the authority of the most qualified kind of poet to praise the hero—an authority based on similarity to him or her—is *competence* (JP 2 1812).

There are many heroes in Kierkegaard's authorship who never or rarely speak for themselves. Some of them, like Abraham, figure prominently throughout a whole book (in the case of Abraham, the book is *Fear and Trembling*). Others appear merely in a brief passage in order to illustrate a point. The most glorious of these heroes, besides Abraham, are Job and Socrates. There is also Christ, who, Kierkegaard explains, is more than a hero. Given that Kierkegaard often says that he writes in order to clarify what Christianity is, and that he thinks Christianity involves faith in Christ, it is remarkable how seldom Kierkegaard describes Christ, or even mentions his name. It seems that Kierkegaard preserves silence out of reverence, lest he chatter when he has no right, or lest he profane what is holy by praising it to scoffers. But I think there is another important reason for his reserve.

Poetry and Heroism

Christianity as understood by Kierkegaard essentially requires an encounter with Christ, which we might call an I-Thou relation, in which a third party may not intervene without being guilty of presumptuous meddling. As we shall see shortly, Kierkegaard thinks that in order to prepare for this encounter it is necessary to imagine it: to imagine Christ, and oneself together with Christ. It seems to me that Kierkegaard is reticent about poetically describing such an encounter so that he may make as much room as possible for readers to imagine this holy *tête-à-tête* for themselves. Kierkegaard exercises and strengthens his readers' capacity to imagine such an encounter, points them in the right direction, and then leaves it to them to be their own poets of the face-to-faith meeting with Christ. As we shall discover in later chapters, there are some important exceptions to Kierkegaard's reserve about Christ, but for the most part he says very little about the centerpiece of Christianity. It is as though a teacher taught a class about the greatest love poems ever written, but refused to help anyone write their own love poetry, or even to read any student compositions, since any genuine instance of the genre in question should be intended only for the eyes of the beloved.

Kierkegaard describes the proper sort of relation to Christ as becoming "contemporary with Christ" (PC 63). The basic idea of this contemporaneity is that you must make yourself as present and close as possible to Christ in order to have a genuine encounter with him. Many things can get in the way of this holy rendezvous. Anyone who lives in Christendom is likely to have heard a lot of chatter about Christ and Christianity, and therefore is likely to see Christ only through a haze of degrading associations, false prejudices, and sluggish habits of thinking and feeling. We have all heard so much drivel about Christ that it is hard for us to see him with fresh eyes, or without a haze of habit and trivializing associations getting in the way. In order to overcome these obstacles, Kierkegaard says that it is necessary to imagine oneself meeting Christ in person as if one knew almost nothing about him. Such an encounter would surely be quite different from the usual way that a modern person is introduced to Christ, in that it would be more intense, more passionate, more momentous, more demanding, and more challenging. It would reveal accurately what is there to be seen. It is the task of the person who thinks rightly about Christianity to attempt to imagine this real-life encounter. Kierkegaard specifically writes that contemporaneity with Christ requires "poetic imagination" (CUP 65). Only such contemporaneity can lead to faith in Christ, or a responsible, that is, properly informed, rejection of Christ. Christ, according to Kierkegaard, is so important that one should either intensely love and rely on him, or intensely reject him. And this intensity comes largely from the right use of imagination.

There is an analogy between contemporaneity with Christ and Kierkegaard's work as an author. He began his authorship with a book about what he regards as the lowest kind of human existence, namely, esthetic existence, which is selfish, hedonistic, immature, and irresponsible. That book, called *Either/Or*, volume one, is attributed to an author who is an esthete. The purpose of Kierkegaard's beginning his authorship in this way is to meet readers where they are—or many of his readers—in order to lead them to where he wants them to go. He has to appeal to their current taste before he can elevate them to a concern for higher things. He must show readers that he understands and appreciates the things that they do, better than they do, before he can entice them to try to understand and appreciate something better. This strategy of meeting readers where they are might be said to require contemporaneity with readers, imagining what it is like to be them, idealizing their mentality, and reflecting back to them their own purified ideal.

The task of a poetical philosophical presentation of a way of life is to help people understand it as much as possible from the inside, and then to provoke them to admire it, or loathe it, or justly assess its worth, with feeling. A second task, say, in Kierkegaard's presentation of Christianity, is to forcibly impress readers with the necessity of choosing to accept it or reject it, so that if they accept it, they will do so with intense resolve. For this to happen the passions and the whole person must be involved. A poetic philosophical presentation is optimally designed to appeal to the whole person so that resolution in decision is possible. A third task, similar to the second, is to help readers who have resolved to embrace Christianity, or something else, say, a seriously ethical life, to live that way of life as an integrated person whose thinking, imagining, feeling, willing, and acting all sing in unison or harmony with one another under the direction of the ideal. Poetic philosophical thinking, being complete and integrated thinking, supports a complete and integrated life consistent with that thinking.

Perhaps you are skeptical about Kierkegaard's claim that it's possible to imagine accurately what it is like to be another person living another kind of life. Perhaps this claim is a mere fantasy produced by Kierkegaard's overheated imagination. He *claims* that he sympathizes accurately with other people's thoughts and feelings, but maybe this is mere illusion. Here is my defense of Kierkegaard. It may be that few or no people can perfectly identify by way of imagination with others. But ordinary human experience shows that human beings can imagine, more or less well, the inner lives of their fellows. Nearly all of us have had the experience of imaginatively understanding another person, or of being imaginatively understood by a sympathetic friend. And if such sympathetic understanding is possible, then it is also possible to develop one's capacity for it by practicing it, and thereby become better at self-othering. Moreover, you can test your understanding of other people almost scientifically, by describing to them what you think their inner lives are like, and then receiving from them either a confirmation of your description of them, or a correction of it. By the way, Kierkegaard seems to be especially good at imagining himself as other people. His various pseudonyms seem convincingly different from one another. It would be hard to detect that the same person wrote *Either/Or*, volume two, and *Fear and Trembling*. I am told that when Kierkegaard's pseudonymous writings are subjected to stylometric tests designed to determine the authorship of ancient texts, the result is that his pseudonyms are pronounced to be different authors.

We can better understand the way in which Kierkegaard is a dialectical poet who presents various ways of life, by comparing him to two kinds of novelists: namely, those who are especially interested in ideas, and those who are concerned to give moral instruction to their readers. I suppose that the similarities between Kierkegaard and these two kinds of novelists are fairly obvious. Therefore I will focus on the crucial differences.

Kierkegaard writes about ideas much more than almost any good novelist does. We would be annoyed with him if we opened his books expecting stories and found a great deal of deep thinking. Kierkegaard is not quite entertaining in the way that a novelist should be, though it is easy to see that he could be novelistically entertaining if he wanted to. Samuel Johnson posits that the purpose of art is to delight and instruct. Most modern theorists of art focus much more on art's delightfulness than on its instructiveness. What is more, many recent art-critics are prone to condemn attempts at art that focus too much on instruction. They think that a didactic agenda spoils artistic execution. It must be admitted that Kierkegaard is far more interested in instructing than in delighting. But he does nonetheless delight as he instructs, because his art overflows everything that he writes.

More often than not when Kierkegaard tells a story, he gives only the outline of its plot, with some commentary. He is quite fertile in plot-ideas. I suppose that if you culled his whole authorship you could find condensed plot-outlines for hundreds of excellent novels. There is a single paragraph in one of Kierkegaard's books, *Fear and Trembling*, which contains at least six or seven variations of a basic plot summary. Kierkegaard's bare-boned plots are surprisingly interesting. They have a sort of mythic quality. Like myths, they are pared down to essentials, and thus leave out details. But their essence has such power that they hauntingly provoke your passions and your imagination.

There are two or three stories in Kierkegaard's authorship that have enough body and details in them to be called novels. They all consist of diaries or letters. Not surprisingly, or rather, exactly as is to be expected, they focus almost entirely on the inner life of one or two persons. If we tried to categorize them as plays, we would have to say that all there is in them are the monologues of the central characters. They are nonetheless dramatic, but the drama is all in the mind of the protagonist, or monotagonist.

These Kierkegaardian epistolary or journalistic novels do not contain many things that most novels do. There is almost no description in them of the social circle of the main character. More generally, they do not attempt to describe the social world as it is. Instead they describe instructive ideal possibilities which are rarely to be met with in the world in their pure form. As I indicated earlier, Kierkegaard thinks that these ideal possibilities are more instructive than actualities, because the question for Kierkegaard is not how to tweak our lives in order to make them a little better, but how to revolutionize them by living for an ideal. There is also very little action in Kierkegaardian novels. And whatever does happen is thoroughly reflected in the mind of the main character. The point is how this character thinks and feels about events, not just the events themselves. A deep life does not need as many events as one might suppose, if a person has a deep relation to his or her deeds. Kierkegaard's protagonists are something like displaced monks, monastics inserted into the world. Most novelists are quite interested in the relations of people to one another. There are to be sure a few interpersonal relations of a sort in Kierkegaard's novels. But with very few exceptions, only the main character speaks or acts. Thus a Kierkegaardian novel is essentially a first-person report of the inner life of one person who does little in the world, but who exemplifies a way of life in his descriptions of his thoughts and feelings about relatively few actions.

We might have expected Kierkegaard to write novels that inspire us by describing people who *grow* personally, ethically, or spiritually. We might have expected coming-of-age stories, or *bildungsromans*. But Kierkegaard does not write such stories. One of his pseudonyms claims that no one is ever "assisted in doing the good" because someone else did it (CUP 359). If this were true, then there would be no point in Kierkegaard's trying to inspire his readers to grow by describing someone else's growth. But I think Kierkegaard's pseudonym exaggerates. It is undeniable that people are sometimes helped to become much better by the inspiring examples of others. Kierkegaard himself sometimes admits this. There is nonetheless a germ of truth in the pseudonym's claim. People can be deeply moved by reading about another person's triumphant conversion to a better way of life, but then make no effort to imitate this conversion themselves. The fictional change of heart then turns out to be a substitute for a real amendment of life. I can feel good about myself because I have such deep feelings about what a real or fictional character did, so that there is no need for me to try to do anything myself. Thus inspiration can degenerate into refined excuse and evasion. Kierkegaard is especially eager to avoid giving anyone an excuse to evade personal struggle for an ideal, and that is probably why he avoids inspirational examples of successful struggling for an ideal, even though what he wants most for his readers is precisely successful struggling for an ideal.

Some of you may be thinking that if Kierkegaard writes much more to instruct his readers than to delight them, his poetic presentation of ideas and ways of life must be annoyingly moralistic and preachy. But they are far from this. His great art prevents it. Moreover, he does not interrupt the self-report of his diary-writers in order to comment on them. As you read the diaries of his representative personae you are invited to try to understand and assess their ways of being and of living. Admittedly, sometimes Kierkegaard provides a commentary or a diagnosis of his heroes and villains. But these analyses come later, and they are not plodding, but artful and interesting. Everything connected with his novels works together to invite readers to experience a way of life from the inside, and to reflect upon the meaning of that way of life, and the possibility of embracing or rejecting it.

In the following chapters we will examine Kierkegaard's poetic presentation of heroes, a villain or two, and their ways of life. In our examination we will see the "great dialectic of life ... exemplified in representative individuals" (EO 2 87). In order to understand and personally encounter these representative individuals, we will need to examine the ideas that guide them. The chief goal of this book, however, is not to explicate Kierkegaard's existential ideas, but to reflect on persons whose lives artfully express these ideas, because, as I have argued, such reflection is the best way to inquire into how to live.

In the next chapter we will examine Kierkegaard's first book, *Either/Or*, volume one, which presents what he calls the "esthetic stage" or *sphere* of human *existence*, and is perhaps his most interesting book, certainly his best-selling book during his lifetime—which is fitting, because the pseudonymous persona who is its fictional author is an esthete who cares about nothing so much as the interesting.

CHAPTER TWO

An Esthetic Fantasy, Kierkegaard-Style

THIS CHAPTER IS A sort of Siren's song, drawing you away from the toil and responsibilities of the workaday world. Like a seducer, I wish to persuade you to indulge in a fantasy, or even multiple fantasies. I invite you to enjoy and explore the time-honored dream that has been dreamed perhaps more times than any other human dream. What would you do, how would you live, if you were extravagantly wealthy? In this fantasy you are not permitted to imagine that you would be noble-minded or generous in the use of your riches. For I do not easily believe it when people who indulge in fantasies of immense wealth boast that they also want to be generous humanitarians. The theme of your dream is not what sort of benefactor of humanity you would be if you were favored with fantastic wealth, but how you would live for yourself, selfishly, and voluptuously, if you had mythical riches at your command.

Let us make the fantasy even more thrilling. Imagine that you were drawn up into the seventh heaven, and appeared before a council of the gods, who offer you the following special dispensation. They will give you not only wealth, but robust health, personal beauty, seductive charm, and, what is most important, a free pass, license, or permission to live as you wish without any threat of divine retribution for immoral behavior. In order to make things still more interesting, it is necessary to set some limits to your fantasy. The following conditions apply to your divine boon. You must be prudent enough in the use of your blessings not to be apprehended by the police and convicted by the judicial system for serious crimes. You must be wise enough not to ruin your health and good looks with riotous living.

An Esthetic Fantasy, Kierkegaard-Style

You must, in other words, be subject to the natural consequences of your actions. The world will punish you for your folly, even in this fantasy, but the gods give their word not to penalize you for immorality. So you are free to live selfishly, seeking pleasure and interesting experiences, acknowledging no absolute ethical laws that would cramp and constrict your choices.

How then would you live? What sort of life would you choose? Notice that the gods in your fantasy did not give you an advisor. But you might need one. The question of how best to take advantage of a voluptuary existence may be much harder than you suppose it is. You might make serious mistakes in attempting it. The philosopher Rousseau is instructive on this point. In his book, *Emile*, at the end of its fourth part, he describes how he would live if he were rich, selfish, and not too concerned about ethics[1]; and his description aptly reveals that sensuous and selfish life is riddled with snares and pitfalls for the unwary, and therefore requires prudence or wisdom.

There are so many possibilities to consider. The very lack of an authority over your choice means that you have many options. You could decide that life is play, and seek amusement or entertainment. Or perhaps you would choose to spend your time creating or enjoying art. Or perhaps you might make use of the hedonistic trinity of sex, drugs, and rock and roll. Or maybe you are more cultured and sophisticated, so that you prefer wine, opera, soirees, and spas. Or maybe you think life as a party would quickly become boring, and that it would add zest to your existence to pursue some sort of goal in competition with other people, in business, say, or politics, athletics, gambling, or war. Or maybe you would live an intellectual life, not in quest of the serious goal of truth, but in pursuit of interesting ideas and conversations—in pursuit, in other words, not of what should be thought, but of what might be said. The first ode of the Roman poet Horace eloquently expresses this multiplicity of possibilities in something like the following words: "Various are the pursuits of men—athletics, politics, agriculture, commerce, epicurean ease, war, the chase. Me the poet's ivy and the muse's cool retreats delight."[2] Finally, you might decide that there is no reason for an amoral sensualist to commit to one line of life over all others, and that you would practice what Kierkegaard calls the "rotation of crops" method: that is, you would seek variety (EO 1 281–300).

---

1. Rousseau, *Emile*, 344–54.

2. Horace, *First Ode*, 139. The quotation is a condensed and paraphrased translation of the first ode of Horace, and seems to be the work of William Broome.

Poetry and Heroism

Before we proceed, I have a word for the grave and upright people among us. Perhaps you judge that our fantasy is frivolous, evil, or unworthy of serious consideration. But, I would reply, this dream is part of human nature itself, and therefore requires examination. Human beings are drawn to this fantasy always and everywhere, even if some exceptional people ultimately reject it. The life of the gods in Homer's *Iliad* and *Odyssey*, which we might well call the collective dream of the ancient Greeks, is very similar to this fantasy. Very serious and sober philosophers assign great importance to pleasure, Plato and Aristotle, for example. Consider Plato for a moment. When he compares the lives of a just person and of an unjust person in the *Republic*, he devotes much of his investigation to the question which life affords a person more pleasure. So you see, Plato does not disdain pleasure, but considers it an important criterion by which to judge the value of possible ways of life. And if pleasure is very important, then our fantasy might be an apt way of inquiring into the nature of pleasure and its role in the good life. Consider the philosopher Immanuel Kant, who is perhaps the most moralistic of all the great thinkers. Having claimed that you ought to do your moral duty with no regard for the pleasure or pain it will bring you, he finds it necessary to hypothesize that there is a God who will reward virtuous people with pleasure and punish evil people with pain in an afterlife. Thus even the arch-moralist Kant ends up doing homage to pleasure. And if even the sage of Konigsberg has his hedonism, then, at the least you should preserve an open mind about the seriousness and usefulness of our fantasy.

At this point I feel the need of assistance, and I am going to summon a philosophical master-fantasizer who can help us in our enterprise, which is half fantasy, half philosophy. This genius of the art of philosophical fantasy is Søren Kierkegaard, of course. His name for living selfishly, for pleasure, and for interesting experiences, without fear of divine retribution for immoral behavior, is the *esthetic stage* or *sphere* of *existence*; and he creates a literary persona who is a virtuoso of esthetic life. This character is the fictional and anonymous author of most of Kierkegaard's first book, *Either/Or*, volume one. Since this character remains unnamed throughout *Either/Or*, we will follow the convention of calling him 'A' (without the continual use of quotation marks—that is A, instead of 'A'—so be on the alert). A speaks for the esthetic sphere of existence from the inside, as someone intimately acquainted with esthetic life, someone who has richly experienced this life, knowingly chosen it in preference to all other lives, and perfected it. He does not just speak about esthetic life, but he exemplifies it, and we as readers of *Either/Or* are invited to imagine ourselves in his place, to imagine, that is, what it would be like to be a genius of esthetic existence.

The presentation of the esthetic sphere of existence given by A in *Either/Or* is exciting, interesting, and tempting. *Either/Or* was Kierkegaard's best-selling book during his lifetime, and for good reason. The presentation of the esthetic in it is so powerful that some intelligent and sensitive readers think Kierkegaard is himself an esthete, even though he explicitly denies this, and identifies himself as belonging to the ethical and religious spheres of existence. But these readers seem to believe that Kierkegaard could not have presented esthetic life so convincingly if he were not himself an esthete. Kierkegaard's descriptions of modes of life, even of modes that he regards as profoundly mistaken, are so appealing that the temptation to appropriate him as an ally is hard to resist.

Given the variety of esthetic lives, it might seem ill-advised for Kierkegaard to represent the esthetic sphere through only one person. Why then does he not allow more characters to speak for the esthetic sphere? There are a few reasons. Kierkegaard regards A as belonging to the most advanced level of esthetic existence. He has passed through all the levels of the esthetic and has arrived at the last one. A is at the esthetic sphere's final stage mainly because he is *reflective*. He reflects on or thinks hard about his esthetic existence. When he was younger he was presumably more naive, more spontaneous, and therefore less reflective about himself and his life. But in his maturity he has experienced and pondered the esthetic from top to bottom. Therefore he is qualified to speak in general for that whole sphere. Another reason that Kierkegaard does not attempt to have other esthetes speak for the esthetic sphere is that most of them simply cannot do this, because they do not understand it or themselves. Naive, unreflective, and spontaneous people cannot speak for their way of life because they do not understand it. They cannot step outside of it in thought in order to contemplate it and consider how best to describe it to other people.

Although there is only one spokesman, or at most two, for esthetic life in *Either/Or*, there are many representatives of it. They simply do not speak at length for themselves. The most memorable of these representative esthetes in *Either/Or* is Don Juan, or, as he is called in Mozart's opera, *Don Giovanni*. In Kierkegaard's terminology, Don Giovanni is *immediate*. In other words, he is unreflective, or not self-aware, and he is uncalculating and spontaneous. In keeping with his unreflective immediacy, he says nary a word in A's chapter on the "immediate erotic." According to A, the best way to communicate immediate esthetic existence is not through words, but through music. He claims further that the perfect musical representation of esthetic existence is Mozart's opera, *Don Giovanni*, and he devotes many pages to interpreting *Don Giovanni* and to using this opera to illustrate three distinct stages of immediate esthetic existence.

By the way, A and Don Juan are mirror images of one another at opposite ends of the esthetic spectrum. Both are lovers of a sort. Both are seducers. But Don Juan's seduction works through the raw power of his erotic vitality, while A's seduction works through thought, cunning, rhetoric, contrivance, and deception. Don Juan overwhelms his victims with the elemental energy of his erotic immediacy. A scientifically studies his victim, manipulates her, skillfully molds her character into the shape he wishes her to assume, and artfully contrives various situations in which to observe and enjoy her, in order to make his conquest as interesting as possible to himself. Given their differing methods, it is fitting that Don Juan has many conquests, by legend 1003 just in Spain, but A has only one, or perhaps at most a few. Therefore A says that Don Juan is an *extensive* seducer, and that he himself is an *intensive* seducer.

Let us begin our exploration of A by examining his strengths, or virtues. What makes him appealing or attractive? What does he get right? What about him might we want to imitate, even if we aspire to go beyond the esthetic sphere? What are the seeds of growth in A if he himself were going to overcome his difficulties in life?

A has great talent, and has carefully cultivated it. He is extraordinarily intelligent and has a flair for art. He is himself a great literary artist with a capacity for keenly appreciating and perspicuously interpreting music and literature. If he did not have these developed talents, he would not be capable of living the life of a reflective esthete with any success. Making and enjoying art are crucial for such a life, as is intelligent and perceptive observation of oneself and others. Possessed of all these esthetic resources, A lives artfully, poetically, beautifully, and above all in an interesting manner. In order to live thus the reflective esthete needs, in addition to intelligence and artistic talent, the leisure and the opportunity to develop his talent, and therefore money. If it is true that esthetic life requires rare abilities, then already we can see that it may not be the best life for most people, since we are not all rich and highly talented.

If A may be said to live well, this is partly because he acutely discerns the defects in conventional life. In one of his Diapsalmata, which are aphorisms near the beginning of *Either/Or*, and which contain in condensed form his major themes, he writes the following: "The most ludicrous of all ludicrous things, it seems to me, is to be busy in the world.... What, after all, do these busy bustlers achieve? Are they not just like that woman who, in a flurry because the house was on fire, rescued the fire tongs? What more, after all, do they salvage from life's conflagration?" (EO 1 25). We see here that A perceives that most people tend to be comically busy bustlers about petty and trivial things which are not worth the effort. This is a great virtue. If he can accurately perceive the unworthiness of some goals, perhaps he can also recognize goals worthy of serious effort.

A finds many things in the world ludicrous, laughs at them, and can aptly reveal their absurdity. Consider the following quotation from his aphorisms: "when I became an adult I opened my eyes and saw actuality, then I started to laugh and have never stopped laughing.... I saw that the meaning of life was to make a living ... that the rich delight of love was to acquire a well-to-do girl, that the blessedness of friendship was to help each other in financial difficulties, that wisdom was whatever the majority assumed it to be, that enthusiasm was to give a speech, that courage was to risk being fined ten dollars, that cordiality was to say "May it do you good" after a meal, that piety was to go to communion once a year. This I saw, and I laughed" (33–34). This passage is brilliant. Each little satirical imitation of conventional mediocrity is quite cutting, and the whole is a tour de force. Not only does A identify many things that might make life worth living, like love, friendship, wisdom, enthusiasm, and piety; he also wittily mocks the superficial meanings attached to these grand ideas by the "bourgeoise philistinism mentality."

Consider the following excerpt from one of A's most potent aphorisms:

> ... let others complain that the times are evil. I complain that they are wretched, for they are without passion. People's thoughts are as thin as lace, and they themselves as pitiable as lace-making girls. The thoughts of their hearts are too wretched to be sinful. It is perhaps possible to regard it as a sin for a worm to nourish such thoughts, but not for a human being, who is created in the image of God. Their desires are staid and dull, their passions drowsy .... Fie on them! That is why my soul always turns back to the Old Testament and to Shakespeare. There one feels that those who speak are still human beings; there they hate, there they love, there they murder the enemy, curse his descendants through all generations—there they sin (28).

In this aphorism A claims that his contemporaries have sunk into a subhuman mode of existence, because their thoughts and passions are pathetically weak and petty. He longs for intensity, even if it is sinful intensity. Would that people were either passionate scoundrels or passionate heroes. But because they are neither villains nor saints, A spews them out of his mouth, and pours forth his scorn and witty abuse upon them.

If A condemns the passionless mediocrity of his times, he also delights in more noble and high-minded versions of humanity. He writes that the story of Aladdin "is so very refreshing because [it] has the audacity of a child, of the genius, in the wildest wishes. Indeed, how many are there in our day who truly dare to wish, dare to desire . . . ? (22). Similarly he writes admiringly of the "poetical power of folk literature," or what he calls its "power to desire." "Desire in folk literature," he writes, "is fully aware that the neighbor does not possess what it seeks any more than it does itself" (22). By poetical desire A means desire for things that are worthy of being celebrated by poetry, that is, desire for the extraordinary, the achingly beautiful, the breathtakingly noble, the romantic, or the sublime. And he praises folk literature for its potent awareness of the human desire for some great thing. The English writer of the sixteenth century named Richard Hooker eloquently describes this desire in the following sentence, whose subject is the human soul: "Somewhat it seeketh, and what that is directly it knoweth not, yet very intentive desire thereof doth so incite it, that all other known delights and pleasures are laid aside, they give place to the search of this but only suspected desire."

Given that A approves of poetical desire, it is not surprising that he also admires heroes, and sometimes fancies himself as one. Drowsy desires, which A mocks, do not produce heroes, but poetic desires, which he praises, sometimes produces them, and may even require heroism. In his essay on Mozart's *Don Giovanni*, A expresses intense admiration for that opera, and even more enthusiastic admiration for Mozart, its creator, whom he looks upon as a hero of musical composition. He gives himself over fully to the logic of admiration, expressing his debt to Mozart, his gratitude for Mozart, and his zeal for spreading the glory of Mozart. It is telling that A admires Mozart more than the opera. This admiration shows the seeds of A's desire to be great. He writes that he is "striving for" an "acknowledgement" of the "absolute validity" of Mozart's *Don Giovanni* (116). It is striking that A uses the phrase *absolute validity*, even if only in an esthetic manner. Someone who can conceive of absolute validity is the sort of person who might eventually be led to transcend a merely esthetic view of life.

An Esthetic Fantasy, Kierkegaard-Style

In order to appreciate another of A's virtues, you need to be apprised of the fictional frame for the publishing of A's papers. According to that fiction, a man named Victor Eremita discovered A's unsigned papers in a mysterious desk, and then edited them for publication. You might suspect that the backstory about A's papers is merely a cute conceit, a superfluous artistic flourish designed to give A's papers an artificial charm. Nothing could be further from the truth. The papers themselves have a sort of subtitle, *ad te ipsum*, which is Latin for, "to himself." A writes to and for himself, not for publication. It is utterly crucial that he does not write for the public, but merely for himself, because this reveals his character and virtue. He does not live through the eyes of others. He does not need their approval in order to enjoy himself. He has his own rich inner life. He has a reality underneath his appearance. He is not a mere mask, but a person behind a mask. He has independent judgment. He thinks for and reflects on himself, with some degree of honesty, seeking self-understanding. In his self-examination, A becomes aware of many problems in his esthetic existence, and he even seeks, maybe half-heartedly, for a solution to these problems. In other books Kierkegaard says that this strong and independent inner life is essential to one of his central ideas, namely, subjectivity. But setting aside jargon, I think we can agree that A is attractive because of his rich interior life, his independence of other people, his partly honest self-examination, and his acknowledgment that his esthetic existence is plagued by various maladies. Being richly subjective as he is, it is fitting that he did not seek to publish his papers, but hid them in the secret compartment of his desk, because he wrote them to and for himself, not for public consumption.

Now that we have generously and sympathetically appreciated and even admired A's esthetic strengths and virtues, let us critically consider the weaknesses that he reveals about esthetic existence. But how are we to go about criticizing and objecting to A's estheticism? We could denounce him moralistically. For his morals are highly objectionable. But this sort of criticism would not be convincing to an esthete like A, who would wittily laugh off our conventional moralism. Nor would this sort of refutation of A be fully convincing even to us, if we have any inclination to be esthetes ourselves. If we want to address whatever in us is attracted to living for interesting and beautiful experiences, it cannot be enough merely to denounce A and his life with righteous indignation. A better method would be to use A's own standards and his own reports of himself, in order to show that he himself is not satisfied with his esthetic life. But of course our goal is not really to convince A, who is after all a fictional character. Our aim is instead to judge for ourselves what our honest reaction is to A's invitation to esthetic existence. In order to judge as well as possible we may end up criticizing A both by his own standards and by ours, even our ethical standards, if they are genuinely ours. More accurately, we want to evaluate estheticism with our whole selves, not just with the ethical part of ourselves.

A is himself concerned about the lack of meaning in his life. He often asks what his life's meaning is, and he complains about the meaninglessness of his existence. Let us consider one of his more remarkable complaints: "My life is utterly meaningless. When I consider its various epochs, my life is like the word *Schnur* in the dictionary, which first of all means a string, and second a daughter in-law. All that is lacking is that in the third place the word *Schnur* means a camel, and in the fourth a whiskbroom." (36). A's aphorism is whimsically comical in its invention of a third and fourth meaning for *Schnur* as a camel and a whiskbroom. But on the whole the aphorism points to a serious flaw in esthetic life. Since the esthete acknowledges no authority over himself, no binding duties, and no weighty responsibilities, it is hard for him to persevere in any one course for long. The result is that his life breaks apart, or that it is fragmentary. He tries one thing, soon grows bored with it, or finds it too difficult, or not sufficiently meaningful, and therefore moves on to something else. His life is indeed a *string* that unravels whenever he attempts to bind his life into a stable configuration.

Esthetic life's lack of profound meaning is surely its greatest weakness. If I pursue only pleasure, amusement, diversion, and interesting experiences, I am likely to feel, with sorrow, and maybe despair, that all this play does not amount to much. Kierkegaard does not fabricate or exaggerate, but is realistic, when he has A himself lament the meaningless of his existence.

A might respond to our criticism by saying that of course it would be wonderful if there existed a great good to live for with devotion and dedication. But he does not see any such sublime good, despite being a very clever fellow with good vision. A implicitly denies that there is a Good in several highly memorable passages.

The last aphorism in his Diapsalmata resembles the fantasy with which we began this chapter. A too is taken up into seventh heaven and encounters all the gods, who grant him a boon. "Choose" they say, "but only one thing." A's response is telling, and I will quote it in full. "For a moment I was bewildered; then I addressed the gods, saying, my esteemed contemporaries. I choose one thing—that I may always have the laughter on my side.

An Esthetic Fantasy, Kierkegaard-Style

Not one of the gods said a word; instead, all of them began to laugh. From that I concluded that my wish was granted and decided that the gods know how to express themselves with good taste, for it would indeed have been inappropriate to reply solemnly 'It is granted to you'" (42–43). This is a rich and ambiguous passage. We see in it A's tendency to be comical and flippant in serious situations. We see that he disrespects the gods by asking them for a seemingly trivial gift. His response to their grand offer reminds me of a story about the cynic Diogenes Laertius. When Alexander the Great, the world-conqueror, approached him and ostentatiously offered him any gift that he wished to choose, Diogenes disrespectfully replied: unshadow me please, you are blocking the sun, and I am sunbathing.

A's jesting response to the imaginary offer of a gift from the gods is based on the implicit claim that there is no great good that the gods could give him. But, we should ask, does A really *know* there is no supreme good? Has he searched diligently for it with all his heart, mind, and strength? Does he reject some possible goods because they require too much work, suffering, and sacrifice? Does he reject God because worshiping God requires humble obedience? I think we can agree there is good reason to be suspicious of A's motives and efforts as a seeker.

It is telling that A does not simply tell the gods that he doubts there is a *summum bonum* which would deeply satisfy him. Instead he asks that the laughter always be on his side. What is the meaning of this request? Someone might answer: "Well, laughing intelligently at ludicrous things is fun and interesting. That's why." But I think there is more to it than that. When we laugh at something, we feel superior to it. We feel that we know or understand that there is something ridiculous about it. When A asks that the laughter always be on his side, he is in effect asserting that he enjoys the sense of his own superiority to other people who base their lives upon comical or illusory goods. He feels superior because he thinks that he shows courage and intelligence in rejecting comforting illusions. I submit that this feeling of brave and intelligent superiority is the meaning of A's life, or a large part of its meaning. He does not give up on meaning and pursue only the interesting. His pursuit of the interesting is based on a secret sense that he is great and heroic by having the laughter always on his side. If I am correct about this, then some important questions emerge. What is the nature and source of the meaning in courageous and intelligent rejection of comforting illusions? If discernment and courage are meaningful, then could there be something more profoundly satisfying than being a courageous genius of irony and satire?

A claims that with regard to every important decision in life, whether you choose one alternative, or the other, you "will regret it either way." For example, whether you "marry or do not marry, you will regret it either way" (38). Obviously this is to say that there is no good great enough to be unregrettable. But A does not stop with that. He says that by not choosing, he is "always *aeterno modo*," that his life displays the "true eternity" (39). It is revealing that it is not sufficient for A himself merely to assert that there is no unregrettable good. He must glorify his way of dealing with this problem in grand words about eternity. This self-glorification is in effect a claim that living *aeterno modo* as he does has serious value. But if this way of living is a serious good, what is the nature of its value, and can this kind of goodness be used to support a better life than one that strategically avoids regrets? If there can be any serious good at all, then maybe there are greater goods. If A were really earnest, he would have investigated this possibility with great zeal.

I have tried to show that A implies that there is deep meaning in his life. But his official position is that there is no profound meaning in his existence, and that he pursues interesting experiences instead of sublime ideals. That is, he tries to substitute the interesting for the good. He has many ways of making life interesting. We can consider only some of them.

One of his tactics is *recollection*. He attempts to enhance reality by recollecting it: "To live in recollection is the most perfect life imaginable; recollection is more richly satisfying than all actuality" (32). Why might this be so? One reason might be that A's recollections are highly selective: he latches on to what he finds interesting and forgets the rest. Another reason is that A creatively revises and enhances the past in order to make it more interesting. He goes even further than this, making choices in life because he sees that they will lead to experiences that will be interesting to recollect, perhaps with some imaginative revision.

It is suggestive that A does not reject reality altogether, say, by choosing to live in fantasies that he reads or creates for himself; but instead he performs raids as it were on reality so that he can recollect something that really happened. I propose that he does not opt for pure fantasy because reality matters to him. Why then does he want his fantasy to have a relish of reality? Is there a foundation to this care that could lead to a more profoundly meaningful engagement with actuality? The fact that A can imagine possibilities that he prefers to actuality suggests that actuality would be more satisfying to him if his imagined possibilities were to be actualized. If so, why not work to bring some of them into existence?

Another of A's strategies for making life interesting is to carefully observe his emotions and moods, and to enjoy them esthetically. Sadness and disappointment are problems. But it is possible to adopt an observer's mentality in order to enjoy them esthetically. This strategy is not A's own invention. I think we are all aware of times when we have tried to enjoy our own sadness esthetically. A does this a lot: he practices the technique of it almost like a Buddhist monk striving for mindfulness—and he is very good at esthetic self-enjoyment. He even enjoys the thought that he might be the unhappiest person. There is a sort of pride in this thought: only a hero could endure being the unhappiest one, and being heroic is an intoxicating thought. More generally, I suspect A finds meaning in the observer's mentality itself. It is meaningful to him to feel that he can rise above life, transcend it, or adopt a sort of divine point of view. By observing his life he feels that he transcends it. But if A's mode of transcendence is possible, what other possible modes of transcendence might there be, and are any of them more worthy of pursuing than A's preferred mode?

A likes to see himself as brave, nobly stoical about his sufferings, and, in short, heroic. And yet almost all of the strategies that he employs to deal with his problems involve a flight from reality. The strategy of recollection is escapist because it dwells in a falsified past instead of in the present, where real life happens. The strategy of enjoying one's moods and thoughts is escapist because it does not struggle with reality, but instead makes jokes and witty observations about it. Thus A is an escape artist jumping ship when there may be important work to be done on board. And since he sees himself as heroic, he himself has reason to be ashamed of his escapism. For a hero does not flee reality. He endures it; struggles with it; or fights vigorously with it in order to make it better, so that if he fails to transform it, he is crushed by it. Therefore, by his own standards A has good reason to feel chagrined due to his cowardly policy of checking out from reality when things get difficult.

What about other people? How do they fit into A's way of life? Not surprisingly, A knows how to use other people to make life more interesting for himself. One relatively innocuous tactic is to play the hiding game, or what another pseudonym calls the "secrecy system": to be secretive, an enigma, a personality hidden behind a mask, a deceiver (EO 2 112). Hiding one's life from others can be a way of intensifying it. Something kept secret gains in importance and interest merely by being a secret. Hence so many novelists add spice to their stories by suggesting there is a secret and then withholding it from the reader (or from a character in the novel) for a long time. Having a secret can make one feel superior to other people. Suggesting a secret, thereby inducing others to seek to find what you suggest but hide, is a way enjoying their feeling of interest in you, and their feeling of inferiority to you because you hold the key to what they seek—if only you can entice them to be curious. Furthermore, a mysterious manner that makes people curious about you and makes them seek for answers is a way of manipulating them, perhaps for a long time, and thus of enjoying one's power over them. The hiding game is not mere frivolity. It implies that knowing things that others do not is important, and that power too is important. But if knowledge, power, and superiority are goods worth pursuing, why is that so, and could there be kinds of knowledge, power, and superiority that are more worthy than the versions of them at play in the hiding game? Furthermore, if it is enjoyable to manipulate human beings and to reveal oneself as superior to them, does this not imply that there is some sort of value in humanity? I like tricking people more than tricking my dog because I have more respect for humans than for pooches. What then is the value in humanity, and could it be that once we understand this value, we would conclude that the best way to live in accordance with it would be something more substantial than mysteriousness in the parlor, or secrecy at a soiree?

The most striking instance of an esthete relating to other people in *Either/Or* is its last chapter, called "The Seducer's Diary," which presents the esthetic sphere of existence in its most extreme form. The diary is esthetics at its peak, if you are excited by the esthetic, or it is esthetics at its most decadent, if you are appalled by it. There is some mystery about "The Seducer's Diary." A claims that he stole it from a man named Johannes. But it seems likely that he himself wrote it. For who can believe the story A tells that he managed to steal the diary of an esthete who, like him, is a literary genius? Who can believe that, in addition to these coincidences, A's papers are subsequently found in the secret compartment of a desk by Victor Eremita, who is something of a writer himself? If you can believe it, then I have an offer to propose to you. Why then does A deny authorship of the diary? Perhaps he would be ashamed to be thought a scoundrel. Or perhaps he thinks he needs to protect himself from the inconvenient consequences of a reputation for villainy. Or perhaps he likes making us curious about his little mystery.

Johannes the seducer writes that "mere possession" matters very little to him. In other words, he does not care a great deal about the sexual act in itself for its own sake. What he cares about instead is something like possessing or conquering the soul of his victim, who in the diary is named Cordelia. Thus he aspires to be something like a demonic possessor, or a vampire, or even God. Toward the end of his relationship with Cordelia he tries to arrange things so as to be "invisibly present to her everywhere," as Christian theology claims that God is invisibly present everywhere in creation (442). He wants Cordelia to be strong and proud, but he also wants her to be his slave. He wants her to resist him vigorously, but he wants to overcome her completely. He wants her to think for herself, and he wants her to think the very particular things that he teaches her to think. To this end he works with extreme subtly to deceive and manipulate her, and he finds the process of deceiving, manipulating, and observing her to be highly interesting. In fact it seems that he cares more for the interesting process of seduction than he does for the finale. But he does mean to conquer her in the end.

Besides being a master of interesting practices, he is also an expert in the theory of the interesting. He writes that the interesting is produced by a perceived "contradiction between the outward appearance and the inner life" (438). Thus we find hints or clues interesting, and foreshadowing in literature, and clothing that partly reveals and partly conceals. The interesting involves something hidden and something secret, but the secret needs to play mysteriously on the surface appearance. The slow unfolding of the hidden is especially interesting. In this regard Johannes posits the following "law for the interesting": "It must gradually become manifest that nevertheless something surprising was implicit in" a seeming mundanity (365).

What then does Johannes find interesting in seducing Cordelia? He writes that the "infinite prosiness of an engagement is precisely the sounding board for the interesting" (368). Let me try to spell this out. Johannes thinks that an engagement in itself is boring. For, he thinks, it is either a stale convention, or an earnest moral commitment, and he does not find either of these things interesting. When Johannes and Cordelia become engaged, she has the impression that the engagement means more to him than it does. But Johannes gradually reveals to her that he regards an engagement as boring and comical. What is more, he teaches her to smile ironically at their engagement and at other things. He watches her slowly become aware of his secret teaching about engagement and marriage. And he finds her gradual enlightenment an interesting process. He enjoys making her laugh at convention and at ethics. Eventually he even manipulates her so that she herself breaks off the engagement, but consents to have sex with him with no intention of getting married.

Let us now return to our difficult quotation. The "infinite prosiness of an engagement is precisely the sounding board for the interesting" because the prosiness of the engagement is in contrast to the secret teaching about engagements that Johannes subtly communicates to Cordelia. Thus Johannes enjoys the interesting contrast between the prosaic and conventional view of an engagement, on the one hand, and a purely esthetic view of sex, on the other, and he especially enjoys slowly revealing this contrast to Cordelia. Put ethically, Johannes delights in corrupting Cordelia, in converting her from a concern for ethical sexuality to a purely esthetic view of sex. He is a seducer not just because he induces Cordelia to have intercourse with him, but, more importantly, because he wins her to an amoral attitude towards something conventionally thought to fall under the jurisdiction of ethics.

After Johannes has succeeded in seducing Cordelia, he abandons her. She is quite distraught, demoralized, and despairing. She feels herself to be the pathetic slave of Johannes. The editor of *Either/Or*, Victor Eremita, claims that he can discern in A a horror over the behavior of the seducer. I myself see very little evidence of this. Moreover, it would be artless and unconvincing if A or Johannes were to openly confess that he was horrified by the seduction of Cordelia. We would feel that Kierkegaard had cheated if in writing *Either/Or* he made A feel appalled by amoral seduction. If Kierkegaard creates a sophisticated amoral seducer, then he must allow that seducer to have a pretty calloused conscience concerning seduction. But we, on the other hand, you and I, are free to admit that we are appalled by the story of seduction. We are free to say that, if the esthetic ultimately means treating other people as mere means to our pleasure, as our prey, as the hapless victims of our need for amusement, and as mere objects to be exploited, then we reject the esthetic and intend to live ethically. By showing us the moral bankruptcy of the esthetic as revealed in seduction, Kierkegaard gives us the opportunity primally to reject the esthetic.

Johannes abandons Cordelia. But he himself, and A too, are also abandoned. For they live alone. Although he never admits he is lonely, it is highly suggestive that A invents for himself heroic companions to whom he pretends to give speeches. These imaginary companions seem to be evidence of a desire for friendship with admiring equals. But of course A cannot have real friends, or acknowledged equals, unless he were to treat his friends as real people, and not just as means to his own selfish pleasure.

Johannes abandons Cordelia, and A treats other people as means to his pleasure, in order to make things interesting. But wouldn't others be more interesting to A if he acknowledged that they were real people like him? There is an obvious tension in the desires of Johannes when he wants to control Cordelia but also wants her to be free. I posit that he wants to control her because of something like pride, and he wants her to be free partly so that she can be interesting. If he were to renounce his proud desire for control, he could enjoy her otherness and her interesting freedom all the more. Similarly, it seems that if A related ethically to other people, if he treated them as having real and free interiors like his own, he would find them even more interesting.

As we near the end of this chapter, I would like to set forth a critique of A's theory of the interesting. In many situations where there is no beauty it is possible to contrive the interesting by playing a hiding game, by speaking mysteriously, or by deceiving and manipulating other people. This fact suggests that the interesting may be a substitute for unavailable beauty. The seeker after the interesting might prefer beauty, but settles instead for the interesting, which he knows how to contrive and to stretch out. Another way of putting the difference between the beautiful and the interesting is to note that the beautiful gives us joy in a way that the interesting does not. It is possible to take malicious and ironic pleasure in something interesting. The interesting thing might be all the more interesting because it appeals to malice or to one's sense for irony. But it seems to me that it is impossible to enjoy beauty maliciously or ironically. It is not for nothing that in Greek the word *kalos* means both beautiful and noble. For the beautiful inspires us with noble feelings. But all too often the interesting appeals to what is base or cynical in us.

The interesting as A defines it consists in discerning or revealing a tension between appearance and reality, and in the gradual overcoming of this tension as reality is disclosed. This definition, however, does not mention the nature of what is hidden and revealed. If what is hidden and then (partly) revealed is irrelevant to the interesting, then A could enjoy life innocently by solving crossword puzzles, riddles, or math problems. The fact that A does not do this shows that the content or matter of interesting situations is important to him. Human life is more interesting to him than trivial puzzles because human things are somehow important to him. Thus he ascribes a worth to the interesting that he steals from ethics.

As we have seen, A cares a great deal about making interesting observations and having interesting experiences. But he also professes that he is "surfeited and bored with everything" (25). And to be bored is the opposite of being interested. And yet if A cares most of all about the interesting, seeks this quality most of all and with great skill, but is nevertheless usually bored, his attempt to live esthetically is clearly a failure. He speaks at length about his boredom in a rather serious way, saying: "How dreadful boredom is," and lamenting that "the only thing [he] lives on is emptiness." Thus he is bored not because of an accident, but because there does not seem to him to be anything of solid worth to pursue. In the same aphorism he asks "what could divert me?" and he answers: he would be diverted "if [he] managed to see a faithfulness that withstood every ordeal, a faith that moved mountains." But, he says, "my soul's poisonous doubt consumes everything. My soul is like the Dead Sea, over which no bird is able to fly; when it has come midway, it sinks down, exhausted, to death and destruction" (37). I will risk using a cliche. If all work and no play makes Jack a very dull boy, all play and no work makes life very dull for Jack once he has grown up. Play is not enough, and for esthetics, there is nothing serious in mortality, but all is mere toys. A speaks of *managing* "to see a faithfulness that withstood every ordeal, a faith that moved mountains." If he really wanted to, he might be able to see such things. But it is a problem that he wants to *see* them, when he should want to have them and *exemplify* them in his own life. If A were willing to strive for them, his life might already have the meaning that it so sadly lacks.

Dostoevsky says that the atheist is inevitably bored with life. In other words, the really interesting is the religious and the ethical. The person who senses the possible existence of hidden ethical and religious ideals, or of God, and the possibility of realizing these ideals in life, is set up for the most interesting life. There is a great contrast between the ideal and the actual, and that is most fascinating. The ethical and religious person can strive to disclose the ideal in his or her actual life, and that would be most engaging. The task of imitating the ideal is the most difficult, so that the struggle to do this can give zest to a whole lifetime. And because what is hidden and then disclosed in ethical and religious life is not some nonsense or triviality, but divine or sublime worth, the interesting in these lives is not the merely interesting, but also the meaningful, the fulfilling, and the highest good.

Now that we have found fault with A, we can blend our praise and our blame of him together. He is to be highly commended for being aware of much that is wrong with him and his way of life. By the end of his book, if not sooner, he has learned that living like a charmed virtuoso for pleasure is not the blessing that naïve people suppose it to be. Hedonistic life quickly or eventually loses its magic. Just as lovers who lack ethical commitment to one another fall out of love, so the hedonist eventually becomes disenchanted with the unrestrained pursuit of pleasure—though he may remain addicted to it, and unaware of anything better to do with himself. His sense of the meaninglessness of his life haunts him and spoils his pleasure. His lack of serious purpose troubles him. He is often bored, and cannot ultimately solve the problem of ennui, but must seek palliatives, which become ever more extreme and even morbid. At his worst the esthete may be transformed into a vampire or evil spirit who has so little life in himself that he must suck it out of others, or demonically possess them, in order to find his existence occasionally interesting. The eternal vitality of Don Juan is a mere fantasy. In real life he grows old, and both he and his victims derive increasingly less pleasure from his conquests. When, at the end of Mozart's opera about him, Don Giovanni is dragged down into hell, this is not a vengeance wreaked on him by a wrathful and prudish providence, but the natural and inevitable consequence of his ultimately bankrupt estheticism. Our esthetic dream has become a nightmare, not because of the threat of a puritanical punishment imposed from without, but owing to its own inner nature and necessities.

In summary, A's esthetic existence has serious problems, not just by ethical standards, but by his own esthetic criteria. In fairness to A, however, we must ask the following: is there any reason to hope for something better than esthetics? Kierkegaard thinks so, and, as he uses A and Johannes the seducer to represent esthetic life from the inside in volume one of *Either/Or*, likewise in volume two of it he uses a fictional character named Judge William to represent the ethical sphere of existence from the inside. Judge William's task is not just to criticize A, but to try to show that ethical life, especially ethical married life, is better than esthetic existence, that ethical marriage can fulfill the desires of the esthetic, that it can preserve what is right about it while correcting what is wrong with it. In other words, William's mission is to show that ethical life is beautiful and interesting, that it is so meaningful that it cannot be reasonably mocked or justly made the butt of ironic observations, that it is passionate and heroic, that it allows a person not to be fragmentary, but to live a whole and integrated life, that it fulfills the poetical power of desire, that it has both undiluted poetry and unadulterated actuality, and that in ethical life you can be happy with actuality and do not need to resort to fantasy, fairy godmothers, or inexplicable boons bestowed by a council of the gods. In the next chapter we will examine Judge William's praise and defense of ethical life.

CHAPTER THREE

The Apology of a Married Man

IN THE TWO VOLUMES of *Either/Or* Kierkegaard stages a debate about sex and its role in the best life. A, the fictitious author of the first volume, speaks for seduction in particular and for esthetic life in general. Judge William stands up for ethical life and for marriage. Their debate is not merely theoretical, but personal. That is, each debater represents and advocates his own way of life. What then is the character of these two kinds of existence? In summary, an esthete such as A pursues pleasure and interesting experiences, without a sense of responsibility to treat other human beings with respect, and without a sense of divinity which deserves and wields authority over all existence. According to A, the person who rightly understands human nature should be a seducer who regards the seduced as prey to be captured, conquered, or ruthlessly exploited. Judge William, for his part, fights under the banner of ethics and marriage, the latter of which he regards as the highest form of ethical existence. According to William, the essence of ethical life is struggling for the good, and he thinks that any sincere struggler (such as himself) can be assured of achieving a great victory.

Given that William is a judge, and an advocate of marriage, you might expect him to be thoroughly conventional in his thinking. For marriage is among the oldest human conventions, and part of the task of a judge is to uphold the customs and conventions of his society. You might also expect William to sermonize moralistically about the goodness of married life and the wickedness of seduction. But in fact he is not especially moralistic; he thinks of himself as unconventional; and seems to be mostly correct in this. Like A, he has disdain for prosaic common sense and for bourgeois "lethargy and slackness" (EO 2 33). Put positively, he agrees with A that the best life must be poetic, passionate, and intense. But he disagrees with A by asserting that the most beautiful, interesting, and poetic life is married life.

The fact that William's task is to argue that marriage is more esthetic and more beautiful than seduction has important consequences for the way that he argues with A. Instead of imposing ethical standards on A that A does not accept, William uses A's own premises to praise marriage and ethical existence. He argues that A's own esthetic standards require him to embrace married life. This way of criticizing another person's ideas is sometimes called immanent criticism, or internal criticism, because the standards employed are immanent or internal to one's opponent's point of view. One indication that William makes use of immanent criticism is that he says A's *attacks* on conventional marriage "contain the truth," but in a way that A himself does not understand (EO 2 29). This suggests that William will try to show that A's criticism of conventional or bourgeois marriage points to the surprising conclusion that A's choice of life should be, not seduction, but marriage rightly understood and properly practiced.

The outcome of the esthetic contest between A and seduction, on the one hand, and William and marriage, on the other, seems obvious and inevitable. Seduction appears to be much more interesting and much more esthetic than marriage. Furthermore, A is more witty, more interesting, more artful, more learned, and, according to another pseudonym, "far superior" to William "as a dialectician" (CUP 253). Finally, William is not content to praise marriage as esthetically superior to seduction, he also favors working for a living over being independently wealthy, and being ordinary over being elite and exceptional. Thus William has many paradoxes to defend, and seemingly few resources with which to defend them. If Vegas were to take bets in this contest concerning the most beautiful and interesting life, the odds would be heavily on the side of A and esthetics. But, as it turns out, A does not simply mop the floor with William, and it is arguable that William acquits himself better in the debate than A does. Let us examine this dramatic contest of lives.

I should be careful not to exaggerate. The game is not totally rigged in favor of A and esthetics. As I indicated in the previous chapter, A himself admits that his way of life has some problems, and that he is unhappy. This honesty about himself makes A vulnerable to attack. Furthermore, most of us are not pure hedonists in pursuit of pleasure and interesting experiences, other people be damned if they get in the way of our selfish plans. Most of us would be appalled at A's story of seduction that illustrates esthetic life, and that describes pitiless torture of a young lady. There is some sort of conscience in most of us that predisposes us to sympathize with William and ethics. Finally, although William is inferior in natural talents to A, he has the advantage of the maturity that he has achieved through a life of ethical struggle. Often the best advisor is not a brilliant and cocky youth, but an older, sober person who has been ripened by a serious and strenuous life, and who has grown wise from his or her tests and trials. Judge William is such a person.

Why does Kierkegaard stage the great debate about how to live in the way that he does? Why does he handicap the ethical and give esthetics a boost? The simple answer is that esthetics has an initial advantage over ethics, and Kierkegaard is simply honest about this. Most people are sure that esthetics is more interesting than ethics, and if Kierkegaard were to gloss over this fact, nothing he said in favor of ethics and against esthetics would be credible. But if William can manage to win the contest, his victory will be highly significant. If esthetics is allowed its natural advantages, but is nevertheless defeated by ethics, then readers can feel sure that their judgment in favor of ethics is solid and well-considered. Since William does not impose his ethical standards on A, but uses the latter's own ideas about himself and his life, the former has the opportunity to show that esthetics self-destructs, and that it contains within itself a dynamism towards ethical life.

William imagines a young man in need of advice on how to live, and challenges A to a contest in advice-giving. Admittedly, A does not actually get to write his own advice. William imagines it for him, and you might think this is unfair. But it seems to me that William accurately represents the sort of counsel that A might give to a young man. A's first piece of advice is to be rich, because a person needs money to live well. This answer is in line with what we know about A, who devotes himself to art and interesting experiences, which devotion requires leisure and luxury. No doubt A would find work to be pedestrian and unartistic. William, on the other hand, argues that there is dignity in work, and heroism in struggling against the obstacles that life throws in the way of people who are constrained to work for a living. Moreover, William continues, the advice to be rich is exceedingly uncharitable, since most people cannot become wealthy even through great effort.

William imagines further advice that A might give to a young man, namely, to discover in himself a *talent*, especially an artistic talent, and to cultivate it so as to become a special individual (277). This advice that William puts in the mouth of A agrees with what we know about A, who values art very highly, and often mocks ordinary people who are neither clever nor accomplished. William replies that this advice concerning talent is just as unkind to most people as the advice to be rich. William proposes an alternative, namely, discovering one's calling or vocation, if possible in one's work, and pursuing that. Understanding one's work as one's calling bestows meaning on it, and helps to make it fulfilling, even if it seems mundane. A traditional way of understanding a calling or a vocation is that it is the work to which one is called by God. If God requires the work, and pays attention to it, this confers infinite meaning upon even seemingly trivial tasks. George Herbert wrote a poem which treats the intention to perform a task for the sake of God as the Elixir, that is, as a remedy for great ills and as a tonic for robust spiritual health. I will quote a stanza of this poem below, and in order for you to make sense of it you need to know two things: that the *clause* to which it refers is "for Thy sake," that is, "for the sake of God," and that when Herbert uses the possessive pronoun, "thy," he is referring to God. Here is the selection from Herbert's poem: "A servant with this clause / Makes drudgery divine. / Who sweeps a room as for thy laws / Makes that and the action fine." This stanza aptly conveys the ethical sentiment of William about the power of vocation to transfigure work into a divine mission watched with concern by the divine spectator.

William imagines one last piece of advice that A might give to the young man, if that young man should have an intention to marry. If A could not dissuade his protegee from marrying, then he would stipulate that the bride should be a "wonder child," a being that he could never grow tired of, because she is like a nymph or a goddess who is ever young, always fresh, continually new minted, and eternally in her esthetic prime (306). William does not exaggerate when he ascribes such advice to A, who fears nothing so much as a pleasure grown stale and old. But A's advice obviously makes a mockery of the young man's intention to marry. William is more kind in his advice, saying that love is enough to transform an ordinary girl into a source of happiness for life. William explains that the ethical has universal norms, and that among the most important of these is that everyone should marry. Given that everyone should marry, there is no need for a wonder child. It is enough to be ordinary oneself and to marry an ordinary person.

Thus ethics rebukes A's elitism and exceptionalism. Ethics teaches that the universally human is what matters, that exceptional talent is unimportant, and that trying to make oneself an exception to universal norms is a sin. Indeed William deliberately and repeatedly refers to the young man as "our hero," thereby indicating that the heroic is within everyone's grasp, that the heroic does not consist in a privileged destiny or extraordinary talent, but in struggle and victory in universal ethical tasks.

A admits that his conception of life requires good fortune, money, talent, and perhaps a wonder girl, and he happens to have two of these gifts himself, namely, wealth and great natural gifts. But, and here is a very important point, he could lose these boons at any time. As fortune gave much to him, so it could take it all away. Most people are not prepared for bad fortune. They naively assume that things will work out, or they manage not to think seriously about unpleasant possibilities. William argues that such people are in despair. They have an ill-founded hope that fortune will smile on them, so that they are not ready for possible misfortunes. If disaster strikes, they will be cast into despair. But, William argues, they were already in despair, even before disaster struck. To be unprepared for calamity, to hide from the possibility of it, is to despair of dealing with it, and therefore to build one's life on swampy ground. In short, it is a desperate expedient to ignore the precariousness of the good things in life.

A, however, is not like most people. He is not naive, and he does not turn a blind eye to the possibility of personal catastrophe. But he also does not strive to arm himself spiritually for disaster, at least not much. Instead he has a plan of escape. He is willing to commit suicide if things get bad enough. This plan also seems to evince despair, or a lack of good hope. Nor is this the last piece of evidence of A's despair. A implicitly admits that he has ideal longings when he praises the poetical power of desire, and he suggests that these desires are important. He does not, however, hope for their realization. But to be without hope for the fulfillment of one's fundamental longings is to despair.

As we shall see, William proposes a cure for A's despair. But before we examine it we need to consider another way of conceiving the relation of William and A. I have staged that relation as a debate or a contest, and I think there is a lot of truth to this. But it is not the whole story. Another aspect of their relation is that they are something like friends. And as a friend William tries to give A helpful advice. William's main response to A's despair is not to triumph over his friend by boasting of his own good hope.

Instead William tries to help A by showing him his despair, and by teaching him a way out of this sad condition. When William offers a diagnosis of A's spiritual illness and a regimen for a cure, he is not merely passing on information to A. He is *addressing* A, person to person (5, 173). He treats A as a person, which is a grand thing to be, with great responsibilities and great powers. He attempts to make A aware of his sublime abilities as a human being, and his responsibility to develop them.

Kierkegaard shows his wisdom in the way that he sets up the relation of the two volumes of *Either/Or*. As you read volume two, it gradually becomes clear that William has not read volume one, which contains A's essays about esthetic life. To be sure, he is acquainted with many of A's ideas, but not through a perusal of the essays of A that we may read in volume one. Moreover, William reports things about A that we do not learn from volume one, things that he presumably learned from conversation with and observation of A. Kierkegaard's way of setting up the relation of William and A is crucial because it keeps things personal. William is not writing an impersonal scholarly response to academic essays by A. Instead he is writing a heartfelt appeal and advice to a person whom he cares about deeply. He is not propounding ideas, but trying to help a fellow human being and a friend. It is also crucial that Judge William is himself a person. He often says 'I,' and it is apparent that a solid and mature personality is behind his first-person utterances. What he says is what he has learned from life's deep sources, not from academic articles disconnected from life. Judge William is attempting to help A become serious about the task of becoming a human self, and the form of William's writing matches his purpose. He writes letters addressed to someone who he thinks needs to take the task of selfhood more seriously. As we read his letters, it is important that we not be mere observers of the appeals and advice that they contain. We must not be voyeurs. Instead we should acknowledge that we are more or less similar to A, and imagine that William is addressing us. Kierkegaard often includes the following epigraph in his books: To That Single Individual. That is, his books are not addressed to the public en masse, but to single individuals. Ultimately, *Either/Or*, volume two is addressed not to A, but to you, and to me, as single individuals.

William's prescription for curing A's despair is homeopathic: he recommends more of the disease. He prescribes that A embrace his despair, that he "[c]hoose despair" (211). One way to understand this advice is that William is simply recommending honesty. If A is in despair, then he should honestly acknowledge it, and let this truthful recognition of his spiritual condition permeate his whole consciousness. But William has more than honesty in mind. According to the judge, choosing despair has great benefits. The first of these is that fully embracing despair consolidates the personality. It makes one a person for the first time. It is a way of taking oneself in hand, of being one with oneself, of using all one's powers for the truth about oneself. William goes further and explains that by becoming a person one discovers the eternal in oneself: one discovers his "eternal validity" (206). This is to say that a human being is created with the capacity to live in the light of ideals that have an undying value. If a person despairs of achieving her ideals, she becomes sick, and in order to be cured she must become deeply aware that she is made for the ideal, and that longing for the ideal is at the heart of her being. This discovery opens up the possibility of venturing to live for the ideal. As long as A does not fully acknowledge his despair, he lives frivolously: he uses his powers to play artistically with life. But by confronting his despair in all its horror, he would activate his greatest powers, namely, the capacity to become deeply aware of the eternal, the capacity to strive for it, and the ability to examine himself in the light of it. In short, for A to choose despair would be for him to focus his whole self on his frustrated ideal longings, thereby discovering his kinship with the ideal, and to distance or separate himself from the circumstances in which he could not realize the ideal, thereby becoming an independent, integral self.

Let us now leave the frightful topic of despair in order to address the beckoning topics of beauty and bliss. William is so daring, or perhaps so deluded, that he claims marriage, properly carried out, is "the most beautiful task given to a human being" (9). But he may not mean exactly what you think. A crucial distinction is required for understanding his meaning. William writes that most people *confuse* "what is esthetically beautiful with what can be presented with esthetic beauty" (133). Marriage, he admits, is difficult to present in works of art with esthetic beauty. It is difficult to write a play or a novel that presents marriage as esthetically beautiful—so difficult that it has almost never been done. But, although it is hard to reveal the beauty of marriage in literature, it does not follow that marriage is not eminently beautiful in real life for married people themselves. It is also hard to make a film about a genius's joy in thinking, but that does not mean that a genius cannot find joy in thinking. Some excellent things do not lend themselves to an artistic presentation, but are nevertheless accessible to most people, especially ethical things. Still, it must be admitted that

William's claim about marriage is a strange one. The experts on beauty, that is, the poets, do not discern the beauty of marriage. How can William make good on such a bold and even outrageous claim?

William observes that art tends to focus on *the moment*. Art is best at portraying things that do not last, that are short-lived, and it is not very good at portraying things as they mature through work. For example, art is not well-equipped to depict the slow progress of an artisan acquiring and perfecting his craft, but for the craftsman himself this long process might be deeply engaging and rewarding. Similarly, art could not easily depict a person trapped in a narrow cell and struggling to preserve her spirits and her sanity, but this person's struggles might be superlatively courageous and heroic. Art is not as rich as life, and in order to make up for its poverty, it concentrates and intensifies life into a moment, or a few moments. It is like my way of eating cold cereal when I was a child. I would save up the sweetened marshmallows in my Lucky Charms, and then eat them quickly in one blissful bite. Art does the same thing, and concentrates beauty and joy into one or a few blissful moments. William points out that the various arts deal more or less well with time. The art that deals least well with it is painting, which either cannot handle time at all, or only barely. Poetry is most successful in handling time, but it cannot succeed as well as life can. When people live for an ideal, the ideal gives joy to the whole of their existence, permeating their whole lives. The ideal permeates life not only at peak moments, but in struggles, and even in failures, if only people remain dedicated to it.

Let us consider how a purpose may pervade the work and struggle to achieve it. Some athletic training is especially painful, and some is tedious. But if the athlete intensely desires to achieve a goal, this desire can transform the training. The training feels like progress, and its goal gives it meaning. At times even the pain of training is somehow joyful or pleasant, because the athlete interprets it as a sign of progress and of his or her dedication to the goal. The same sort of thing can happen in many other aspects of life. The businessman may enjoy a tedious task because of the thought of the wealth that he hopes to win through it. Similarly with marriage. The ideal of marriage benignly haunts the marriage for those who are serious about it, and gives meaning and joy to all or most parts of the marriage process.

William points out that many famous conquerors in history either could not preserve what they conquered, or could not enjoy their possession. But there might be more excellence in ruling a state wisely and happily than in conquering it. Certainly it does more good to the people in a state to rule it wisely than to conquer it. And yet history has a way of honoring the conquerors more than the wise rulers. We have a bias in favor of conquest. We are not always profound enough to appreciate wise and virtuous possession as it deserves to be appreciated. These observations on conquering and possession obviously apply to eros, with seduction or courtship as conquering eros, and marriage as possessing eros. William argues that just as there is a distinction between "conquering natures and possessing ones" in war and politics, so there is a distinction between them in sex. The conqueror can hold on to the ideal only for a moment (130–31). For the conqueror is like an artist. He empties out life in order to turn it into momentary art. But the married person is a possessor, who fills up life with the ideal in order to make it lastingly beautiful and joyous. This permeating of the actual with the ideal is what William means by beauty (131–33). A should be deeply moved by this possibility. For he himself finds beautiful art in the unity of contrasting elements. And since no compossible elements are more contrasting than actuality and ideality, no beauty is more beautiful than their synthesis.

But what, you may be asking, is the ideal of marriage, and where does it come from? William plays by the rules of immanent criticism and obtains the ideal of marriage from A himself. A writes at length about something he calls "the first love." The first love is the experience of love at the beginning of romance. It is falling in love, and the poetry of life while the bliss of this first love persists. Besides being intense, the first love is poetic; it is a kind of enchantment. A in one way gives the first love its due, by conceding that it is wonderful while it lasts. But, he points out, with a sort of grim satisfaction, it does not last for long. It begins with illusions, he claims, and therefore ends in disappointment.

Judge William argues that marriage, rightly conducted, is the *transfiguration* of the first love (31). Marriage preserves, transforms, and elevates the first love, which is transfigured, not by an alien magic imposed on it from without, but by the growth of an internal principle. The first love is perfected not by candy coating, but by ripening and fermentation that is assisted by ethical husbandry. Let us consider William's treatise on husbandry. According to the judge, the first love aspires to be eternal, and therefore has the eternal within itself *in potentia*. One sign of this is that the lovers feel that they were destined for one another, that they were made for one another, that from the foundation of the world their names were written on the same line on the same page in the book of life. They feel that God or the cosmos created or fated them for one another, and thus their love has for them an eternal and cosmic significance. The lovers also desire their love to continue for eternity. They desire this so eagerly that they voluntarily make oaths to one another of undying fidelity. Duty is often thought to be onerous and deadening. But the lovers feel that their duty to be faithful is a magic spell assisting them to do what they desire more than anything else to do. The eternal is present in the first love also in that the lovers want to thank someone or something for their love, and since for them their love has the highest meaning, they want to thank the highest thing they can for it, that is, an eternal God. Love's feeling of connection with the eternal and the divine gives it joy and meaning.

"All this poetic exuberance about the first love is wonderful," you might say, "but doesn't honesty require us to admit that the first love fails to live up to its grand promise?" "Not necessarily, and not always," Judge William responds. "Some marriages beautifully preserve and transfigure the first love. And if some can, then many more could too, or even all." In order to defend his claim that all people can succeed in marriage, William calls on God for help, and requires married people to do the same. Married couples, he says, should be religiously mature in a way that makes them take their oath of fidelity to one another very seriously (89). If they deeply believe in God and promise before God to be faithful, this will surely help them immensely to fulfill the aspirations of the first love. Mere belief in God, however, is not enough. There must also be a God who actually helps those who pray for help to fulfill their oaths. If God smiles on and supports all sincere efforts at conjugal success, then of course there is good reason to hope that one's marriage will be a blessed transfiguration of the first love. But if there is not such a God, or if God does not care quite as much about marriage as William does, many conjugal unions are doomed to fail in their striving to live up to the ideals of the first love.

Let us examine more fully the problems with William's teaching about marriage. His basic defect is that he is not only idealistic but also triumphalist: he describes ethics both as imitation of ideals and as victorious in this imitation. There are many reasons to doubt this triumphalist idealism. Consider what William says about vocation. He posits as a universal norm that everyone should have a calling. But some people might be so without talent, or so desperately in need of money, that it is hard for them to find meaningful work. Sometimes or often the external conditions of the world do not offer many opportunities for serious pursuit of a vocation, so that myriads of people are forced into horrid working conditions, like England's "dark satanic mills" of the nineteenth century. When he teaches that everyone must find a vocation and fulfill it, William compounds the misery of people who cannot find or fulfill their vocation, by suggesting that they are somehow *guilty* (217).

The most important universal norm for William is that everyone should marry. If he is right that there is such a universal requirement, surely this will result in misery for many people. Some people will have unfaithful spouses. If the meaning of life is marriage, then having an unfaithful spouse would be a source of great misery. There are also people who do not feel drawn to marry, who therefore will be made unhappy by a sense that they have a duty to marry. There are also unfortunate people whose beloved does not reciprocate their love. William himself speaks vaguely of some people whose lives are too *entangled* to marry (117). Perhaps he means some people have problems which would be wrong to share with another person, problems such as melancholy, crushing debt, a debilitating disease, or onerous family obligations; or, if we get fantastic, a person might be the object of a vendetta that would put his spouse's life in jeopardy. Thus the teaching that everyone should marry contributes to the unhappiness of people who want to marry, but cannot, by making them guilty for their bad luck.

William triumphantly implies that he, at least, satisfactorily lives up to the ideal of marriage. But ideals are standards of perfection. Does William seriously judge that he achieves perfection? No, for he speaks of guilt and repentance as the common lot of humanity. But if his standards require perfection, and he does not achieve perfection, what right does he have to claim victory? He seems to think that he can make good his failure to achieve perfection—his *guilt* as he calls it—by repentance. Without going into William's theory of repentance, which is a little vague, we can see that it is not obvious that a person of whom perfection is demanded can atone for his guilt and make things good again by repenting. If, as William himself thinks, God is concerned about human guilt, then we need to know God's ways of dealing with guilt. But William is vague about this, and, I think, overly optimistic.

William makes the bold claim that esthetics, ethics, and the religious are "three great allies," that can exist in perfect harmony (147). This claim seems obviously false, or exaggerated. Sometimes ethics requires a sacrifice of esthetic values. The Bible seems to teach that religion can require a sacrifice even of ethical values, as in the case of Abraham, whom God commanded to sacrifice his son. Jesus often talks about the need for painful sacrifices. For example, he speaks of *cutting off* your *right hand* if it *offends you*, and of people who make themselves *eunuchs* for the sake of the "kingdom of heaven."[1] Therefore the differences among esthetics, ethics, and the religious means that they at least sometimes sadly or tragically conflict. But William will have none of this. He is a stubbornly anti-tragic fellow who turns a blind eye to some of the darker and bleaker features of human existence.

William is able to pretend there is harmony between religion and marriage at the cost of being inconsistent in his ideas about God. Sometimes it suits him to regard God as the greatest good who lends prestige to marriage by commanding and supporting it. But he also sometimes treats marriage as the greatest good, and God as subordinate to marriage. For example, he claims that in marriage an ethical person is "infinitely secure within himself" (255). But if a married person needs God's help to make marriage succeed, as William himself insists, then no mere human being can be infinitely secure in himself. At most he could be infinitely secure in God. Similarly, William says that he is happy in knowing that he is *everything* to his *wife* (81). But if God exists, then surely William should be modest enough not to be everything to his wife, since that way lies idolatry. Finally, he writes that "what you are seeking is here," presumably here in the marital paradise (323). But if God is not at any human being's beck and call, but the greatest good to be sought with all one's heart and mind, then how could it be that everything a person wants is here? Thus William treats God as the greatest good when it suits him, and treats God as a servant of marriage when it is convenient to do so. And that is not good theology, or even good logic.

The ending of *Either/Or* contains yet another proof of William's irrationality about God and ethics. The judge appends to his two letters to A about marriage a sermon written by a pastor, and he seems to think that the pastor agrees with him about ethics and marriage. But in fact the pastor is much more focused on God than William is. That cleric's main idea is that "a human being" is "always in the wrong" "in relation to God," and he claims that this thought is *upbuilding*. According to him, no one fulfills his ethical duties, so that no one is in the right in relation to God, and no one

---

1. Matt 5:30, 19:12.

may reasonably regard himself as ethically triumphant (339–54). But, as we have seen, the judge regards both himself and right-living married people as ethically victorious. Somehow William manages not to notice this important and fundamental disagreement between his ethics and the pastor's religion. It seems that his idolatry of marriage has addled his wits, or even made him a bit dishonest.

Despite not achieving the victory for himself that he boasts of, William succeeds in showing that A is in despair, and he points out several inconsistencies and absurdities in A's way of life. For example, he exposes the emptiness of A's "secrecy system," which consists in talking mysteriously about a triviality as though it were substantial, in order to enjoy piquing the curiosity of other people (112). It is pathetic to want to seem to have something substantial to say or to do, when in fact one has only trivialities. William also shows that in some ways ethical life is more esthetic than esthetic life. For example, the person who respects other people and does not try to control and exploit them, leaves them free to surprise him in interesting ways. The esthete, who tries to manipulate other people for his own advantage, hampers their freedom and in this way makes them less interesting than they would be otherwise. Thus the esthete's treatment of other people works counter to his craving for interesting experiences.

William also has a lot going for him. He is an authentic person, a being with a substantial self, which is heroic, free, and responsible. He has eternal ideals, and he makes his life meaningful, beautiful, and interesting by striving for them. He is not selfish. His being is not a cramped being for self, but an enlarged being for self and others—or a being for *us*, that is, himself and his wife.

Even though William's ethical existence is impressive in many ways, it is also marred by many flaws. Neither his ethical teaching nor his practice is consistent. Moreover, he is guilty of many of the same faults for which he reproaches A. William severely criticizes A because the latter's advice is not helpful to a poor and ordinary human being. But it turns out that William's advice is similarly unhelpful to the many human beings who for one reason or another are not suited for marriage. On this point William is even worse in a way than A. For whereas A does not require esthetic life of everyone, William demands that everyone embrace ethical life and marriage. Thus William turns out to be cruel when he burdens people with duties that are impossible for them to fulfill; and because he reproaches A for his inhumane elitism, but is an inhumane elitist himself, Judge William is something very like a hypocrite. Finally William shows that A is in despair. But it is arguable that he himself is in despair too, since he acknowledges ideals of perfection, admits that he does not live up to them, but also needs to sing a victory song in praise of his own life. If William needs to feel victorious in life, but is actually defeated in life, then the proper term for his condition is despair. What is more, if he is in despair, but does not know it or admit it, then he is also deluded or self-deceived.

In short William's ethical life view founders on three things: his teaching about God, his guilt, and his insistence on universal norms. Therefore we might expect to read in later books of Kierkegaard a more adequate teaching than William's about God, a solution to the problem of guilt, and how to become a single individual instead of a standard issue replica of the universal. It is well to keep in mind these three important questions as you continue your study of Kierkegaard, even though we cannot thoroughly investigate them here in this introductory book.

CHAPTER FOUR

The Poet and the Hero of Faith

IN THE LAST CHAPTER we considered Judge William's claim that all people have a duty to marry the one they love, and that by ethical effort in marriage, (virtually) all people can achieve the "most beautiful victory." Johannes de silentio, the pseudonymous author of *Fear and Trembling*, makes the simple and obvious objection to William that sometimes it is impossible to marry the one you love. He imagines a "young lad who falls in love with a princess, and this love is the entire substance of his life, and yet the relation is such that it cannot possibly be realized, cannot possibly be translated from ideality to reality" (FT 41). Perhaps the lad is a peasant, and the kingly father of the princess refuses to allow her to marry someone who is low born. Or perhaps the princess herself does not return the lad's love. There are many possible reasons why people might not be able to marry as they would like. Let us consider an especially dreadful case.

In the book of *Tobit* there is a girl, Sarah, who "knows that the evil demon who loves her will kill her bridegroom on the wedding night" (102). Silentio comments that it is "grievous not to find the person to whom one can give oneself, but it is *unspeakably* grievous not to be able to give oneself" for some reason or other, say, because it would be harmful to the beloved. He adds that owing to her curse Sarah is "defrauded of everything" (103). As interpreted by Silentio, Sarah agrees with Judge William that the meaning of life for her should be to marry and give herself devotedly to her husband. But she is defrauded of the opportunity to do this owing to the violent jealousy of the evil demon. Perhaps jealous demons are rare. But misfortune is not. Many people find it impossible to give themselves in marriage to the one they love, and are thus "defrauded of everything" like Sarah.

Silentio compares Sarah to the title character of Shakespeare's *Richard III*, who, Silentio says, is a *demoniac* because of his "inability to bear the sympathy heaped on him from childhood" for his physical deformity. Silentio comments that Richard's "monologue in the first act . . . has more value than all the systems of morality, which have no intimation of the nightmares of existence" (105). In these words we can hear Kierkegaard responding to the ethicist Judge William, who ignores the nightmares of existence, and naively assumes that (virtually) all people can marry the one they love. Here is the part of Richard's speech quoted by Silentio:

> I, that am rudely stamp'd, and want love's majesty
> To strut before a wanton ambling nymph;
> I, that am curtail'd of this fair proportion,
> Cheated of feature by dissembling Nature,
> Deform'd, unfinish'd, sent before my time
> Into this breathing world, scarce half made up,
> And that so lamely and unfashionable
> That dogs bark at me as I halt by them.

In these eloquent and psychologically matchless words we encounter a person cheated by nature of the love and romance that he craves, and whose resulting anguish is so great that he becomes a scourge for the more fortunate people who either pity or mock him, but do not relate to him with respect as a fellow human being. I think that we can agree that Judge William's optimistic philosophy of marriage does not do justice to the plight of Richard.

"Ethics," says Silentio, "only makes sport of" people like Richard, "just as it would be a taunting of Sarah for ethics to say to her: Why do you not express the universal and get married?" Silentio adds that "[n]atures such as those" of Richard and Sarah are "basically in the paradox . . . either lost in the demonic paradox or saved in the divine paradox" (106). It is impossible in some terrible misfortunes to live as an ordinary human being by taking ethical advice such as that of William. Stronger medicine than ethics is needed for people who are cast out of the human fold by nature or fate. If they do not receive divine aid, they are in danger of becoming *demonic*, that is, proudly disdainful and resentful of the smug contentment of their neighbors. Silentio describes the misfortune of "malformed creatures," saying that "no doubt everyone has an inclination, when he sees the malformed person, to attach to him the idea of moral depravity. What a glaring injustice, since the relation ought to be turned around: existence itself has damaged them, just as a stepmother makes the children perverse" (106). Thus people who are defrauded of everything through no fault of their own tend to be misunderstood and judged unfairly by more fortunate people. Judge William himself in effect does this, by implicitly blaming people who are excluded from marriage, and by not giving them adequate advice and comfort to help them in their misfortune.

Another problem with the ethical theory of Judge William is that it does not do justice to the fact that all people become guilty by failing to do their duty. Admittedly, William proposes *repentance* as the solution to the problem of guilt. Silentio, however, claims that "ethics founders . . . on repentance, for repentance is the highest ethical expression, but precisely as such it is the deepest ethical self-contradiction" (98). What then is the contradiction? On the one hand, William ascribes infinite importance to ethical ideals and duties so that they can make life beautiful and profoundly meaningful for us. But then, when the problem arises that we fail to live up to these infinitely important ideals or duties, William inconsistently does not give infinite weight to our breach of duty. But if, contra William, we place infinite emphasis on our guilt, what anguish is ours. Then we have need of a "guiding star that saves the anguished," and there is no such star in the ethical astronomy of William (21). But there is one in Silentio's.

Let us return to the lad who made his love for an unattainable princess the whole meaning of his life. Silentio says that "the slaves of the finite, the frogs in the swamp of life, scream: That kind of love is foolishness; the rich brewer's widow is just as good and solid a match" (41–42). Silentio dismisses them, saying, "Let them go on croaking in the swamp" (42). The fatal flaw of these frog-like folk is that they lack poetry. They do not have a poetic awareness of sublime ideals that can make life meaningful. Consequently, they lack seriousness, so that they are "continually running errands in life" (43).

To say that people are frogs in the swamp of life, and merely running errands, is comical criticism. But to live without poetry, however cozily and complacently, is to be tragically demoralized. Silentio points out that in the modern world, with its lack of poetry, many people feel that human existence is *empty* of meaning and "devoid of consolation." It seems to them that an inescapable and "eternal oblivion, perpetually hungry, lurk[ing] for its prey," awaits all of us. Nothing will be remembered, and perhaps nothing is really worth remembering. Worst of all, some people suspect that life is ultimately nothing but a cause for *despair* (15). Silentio responds that in order to cure despair, "God created the hero and the poet" (15). The hero is a symbol of ideals worth living and dying for, if only we can see the hero rightly. The poet's function is to help us to attain this correct vision. The poet reveals that the ideals have a "primal lyrical validity" (34). He attempts to inspire a *romanticism* without which we have *sold* our *souls* in exchange for dust or chaff (49). He also attempts to encourage people by giving them a sense of their potential, their dignity, their high calling, and their "eternal validity" as human beings created in the divine image (46).

I am still worried about the lad, and perhaps you are too. Judge William commanded him to make his love for the princess the meaning of his life, and to marry her. But what is the lad to do when marriage with the princess turns out to be impossible? William of course bids the young man to remain true to his love. But, if married life is the best human task, then William's advice excludes the lad from the best life. Moreover, cruelly or negligently, William has little to say about life without the princess. Silentio is wiser and more kind than William. He agrees with William that it was beautiful and noble for the lad to make his love for the princess the whole substance of his life, and that it is right for the lad to remain true when he learns that the princess is unattainable. But Silentio differs from William in that he describes a good life without the princess.

This life is a heroic and poetic one, and Silentio dubs the one who lives it a "knight of infinite resignation." In the forms of human existence recommended by A, Judge William, and Silentio, one constant is the importance of "the first love," which is the enchanted condition in which lovers feel that their love has an eternal significance, and feel therefore a summons to promise eternal and unconditional fidelity to one another. A, the esthete, acknowledges this phenomenon, but thinks it is based on illusion, and recommends ways of exploiting romantic enchantment for esthetic purposes. Judge William, the ethicist, makes this experience the foundation of ethical, married life, and bids the lovers to embrace the intimations of eternity in it by making oaths to one another. Silentio, who is a knight of infinite resignation, agrees with William that the oaths ought to be solemnly pledged, and agrees with A in thinking that there is a good chance that things will not work out for the oath-makers, so that a person needs to have a life-plan that is adequate for coping with misfortune in love.

If the lad who is disappointed in love follows Silentio's advice, how then will he live? First of all he faces facts honestly: he "passionately acknowledge[s] the impossibility with his whole heart and soul" (47). To do this is to admit the limits of his own power, of his hold on any finite good, and to admit that all finite goods are fragile, precarious, and mortal. In other words, infinite resignation is an acknowledgment of one's own weakness and of the fragility of the good things of this world. Despite the impossibility of life with the princess, the young man remains true to his love for her: he "does not contradict himself" (47). Since his love has for him an eternal and unconditional significance, he remains loyal to it and honors it, no matter what. Since the young man lives poetically, and does not want to think one thing and feel another, he is not faithful merely in thought, but also in feeling. "He feels a blissful delight in letting love palpate in every nerve," he achieves "passionate concentration" in his disappointed love (43). Obviously, living like this is painful. But the lad also finds "peace and rest and comfort in the pain" (44). This is because he knows that he has remained nobly and courageously loyal to his love. He has not sunk into the swamp of life, but founded his existence on the firm foundation of service to an ideal. Although he acknowledges his weakness in one respect, he discovers a heroic power in himself to remain true to his love despite immense difficulty. Silentio says that the knight discovers his "eternal validity" as a human being, and his "eternal consciousness" (48). His eternal consciousness is his ability to be poetically aware of eternal ideals, and his eternal validity is his capacity to relate himself absolutely to these ideals. Thus the knight of infinite resignation has a kind of pride, and feels high-minded *disdain* for the "bourgeois philistinism" that he sees all about him.

Although the lad finds peace in his pain, and pride in his endurance of it, he does take one measure to mitigate his suffering. Silentio says that "even in loving another person one ought to be sufficient to oneself." The lad who is a knight of infinite resignation "is no longer finitely concerned about what the princess does" (44). This is to say that he takes a sort of pride in his self-sufficiency, and that he becomes a little distant or detached from the princess. He nobly suffers his deprivation, but he does not invite additional misery by keeping hope alive at the risk of continual disappointment. We might say that he chickens out. But how then does he love the princess whom he renounces? Silentio answers thus: "His love for that princess would become for him the expression of an eternal love, would assume a religious character, would be transfigured into love of the eternal being" (43). To put the point simply, he makes the princess a symbol of God, and he loves God through her image. Although Silentio speaks of a change in the lad's love for the princess when the lad "acknowledges the impossibility," it is arguable his love was always a love of God, without the lad's knowing it. For to give eternal worth to one's love for a mortal creature is a kind of idolatry. We saw that Judge William was guilty of making an idol of marriage. This is the natural idolatry of love, to give infinite worth and meaning to love of a finite beloved. Infinite resignation partly overcomes this idolatry by becoming aware that the princess, or whatever the lost good thing may be, seems so important because she is a symbol.

Although Silentio does not say this, if the knight of infinite resignation manages not to resent the loss of the princess, then, it seems, he must understand that he does not have a *right* to the princess, because she is a gift. Moreover, she is not a gift that he slowly comes to own, but she remains a gift for every moment they are together. As long as he has her, he does so by the renewal of the gift, and if he loses her he has not lost his property, but a generous loan that has not been renewed.

Let us add a few nuances to our account of infinite resignation. Infinite resignation does not have to be based on romantic love. Silentio says that "any other interest" besides romantic love, "in which an individual has concentrated the whole reality of actuality can, if it proves to be unrealizable, prompt the movement of resignation" (41). We see in this quotation that Silentio does not idolize romantic love like Judge William. An important result of Silentio's refusal to idolize romance is that he regards infinite resignation as possible for everyone, not just for romantic lovers. William focuses on giving advice to males. Silentio, however, says of "the order of knighthood" of infinite resignation that "everyone is a member who has to the courage to enroll oneself," both men and women (45). Thus Silentio outdoes William by describing a heroic way of life equally available to all people who are honest about the limits of their power and about the fragility of all finite things.

Given the fragility of all finite things, one might choose to undertake the movement of infinite resignation before misfortune strikes. And since honesty bids us to admit that we have no secure hold on anything, our resignation might embrace the whole world. That is, we could or should *renounce* "the whole temporal realm" (49). This renunciation can include not just the whole world, but all of time as well. At its acme infinite resignation is "every moment to see the sword hanging over the beloved's head" (50). It is not a one and done heroic deed, but a constantly renewed heroic resolution.

The Poet and the Hero of Faith

Although Silentio's ideal is greater in many ways than William's, it nonetheless has serious flaws. Knights of infinite resignation live as *strangers* and "aliens in the world" (50, 41). But surely it is better to love the world and be involved with it than to be detached from it. Knights of infinite resignation love their beloveds not quite as individuals, but as symbols of the eternal. But would it not be better for the knights to love their beloveds as individuals? Certainly their beloveds desire to be loved thus. Presumably the knights love themselves as individuals, and justice requires treating others as one treats oneself, so that the knights should love their beloveds as irreplaceable individuals. There is also a danger in the pride of knights of infinite resignation. Their pride is in one way a good thing, since it shows their awareness of their high calling and eternal validity. But pride easily slips into excess. Furthermore, knights of infinite resignation feel peace and rest and comfort in their pain. This sounds dangerously similar to taking pleasure in self-pity, and could easily degenerate into self-pity if it is not already that from the beginning.

The knight of infinite resignation believes in God, and believes that God can work miracles, but does not ask God for a miraculous gift of the thing that proved impossible for the knight to achieve on his own. But why not ask for help? Silentio says that for a noble nature "it is far more difficult to receive than to give" (104). Perhaps then the knight of resignation is too proud to pray and receive. Perhaps his habit of noble self-reliance prevents him from accepting divine assistance. Thus he seems to be lacking in humility. Or perhaps he is afraid to ask God for a miraculous gift, because it is too painful for him to hold on to the hope that his prayer will be answered, and easier to renounce his desire once and for all. If so, then he is deficient in courage, and by refusing to hope he is in despair. Silentio suggests that this proud despair is *demonic*, and asserts that "there is ever so much more good in a demoniac than in superficial people (96). There is considerable evidence, which you may search out if you wish, that John of silence, who is officially a knight of infinite resignation, hides in his silence a demonic secret.

Silentio both describes and exemplifies infinite resignation. But exemplifying resignation is not his most important function. He is a poet, and the *task* of a poet is "to use his song and speech so that all may admire the hero as he does" (15). That is, his function is to praise his hero, the knight of faith, who for him is represented by Abraham, the Hebrew patriarch, and the father of faith. Silentio even suggests that his "very being" is to praise greatness, especially the greatness of faith (64). Let us see what is praiseworthy in faith according to Silentio.

Faith includes infinite resignation as its first movement, and adds a second, even greater, movement, which corrects and complements infinite resignation, and consists in "getting back" what one has renounced, be it a person or the whole world (36, 49). Getting things back means loving them, not as symbols, but as individuals who are *gifts* from God. It means being involved with people and the world, and delighting in them. It means loving someone as fully as possible and taking the risk that you may lose him or her. Whereas infinite resignation is too proud to receive divine assistance in order to accomplish all these things, faith humbly accepts it.

Much of the greatness of faith consists in renouncing things and getting them back. The knight of faith is better able to do without things than anyone else, and better able to love, enjoy, and appreciate things when he or she has them. Knights of faith acknowledge their weakness, that the good things they enjoy are gifts, not rights, and that these gifts are fragile or precarious. Despite this acknowledgment, they do not detach from things in the way that knights of infinite resignation do, but remain thoroughly involved with them. Making both these movements simultaneously is so difficult that it cannot be done without divine assistance. The knight of faith humbly relies on this assistance, not in a lazy way, but with infinite effort, as though everything depended on him. Nor do they merely rely on divine help; they boldly ask for it, and almost insist on it. Although knights of faith are humble, they also have the "paradoxical and humble courage" to insist on good gifts from God, to importune God like the widow in the parable (49).

Abraham does not merely renounce Isaac. He sets out to sacrifice him, in obedience to the terrible divine command. More generally, the knight of faith relativizes her ethical relation to other people, because she "relates . . . absolutely to the absolute" (70). This is the famous, or infamous, "teleological suspension of the ethical" (54–67). The knight subordinates duties to other people to her relation to God, and for that sake of that relation sometimes even suspends her merely human duties. But even as she does this, or because she does it, she loves people all the more. As Richard Lovelace says to his beloved, "I could not love thee, dear, so much, loved I not honor more," the knight of faith says to his beloved that he loves her as much as he does only because he loves God most of all.

And yet there is a mystery in how one could love someone more by being willing to sacrifice them at the altar to God. Silentio says it is "the most difficult of all and greatest of all" to "remain true to one's love" for Isaac and to God when one is willing to sacrifice Isaac to God. Under the weight of this tension human nature collapses. In order to make such a sacrifice, a mere human being would shed some of his love either for Isaac or for God. But Abraham remains perfectly true to his love for both. For he believes that God is love, that God loves him and Isaac, that if he obeys the command, God will make things work out best for him and for Isaac, and that if he proves his obedience in his ordeal, either God will not in the end demand the sacrifice, or he will restore Isaac to him from the dead.

In summary, the knight of faith "exist[s] in such a way that [his] contrast to existence constantly expresses itself as the most beautiful and secure harmony with it" (50). The knight of faith "absolutely express[es] the sublime in the pedestrian . . . and this is the one and only marvel" (41). Silentio also says that the knight of faith is the "only happy" person (50). This happiness comes from having it all, God and salvation, but also finitude, the world, the princess, a family, a vocation, this present moment, and whatever earthly things one should be grateful for, as gifts from God. But he buys this happiness at the high price of being continually subject to the test of faith.

Silentio comments on his task as a poet by saying that "the point is to perceive the greatness of what Abraham did" (53). The word "perceive" is crucial. Kierkegaard writes that "the portrayal of the existential"—and faith is something *existential*—"is chiefly either realization in life or poetic presentation, *loquere ut videam* [speak so that I may see]" (JP 1 1058). Putting together the statements of Silentio and Kierkegaard, we can say that Silentio praises faith so that we can perceive or see its greatness.

In order to help us perceive the greatness of faith, Silentio thinks that it is insufficient for him merely to praise faith brilliantly. As he sees it, many of his readers are reluctant or else unqualified to admire faith. He says that the present age has "crossed out passion in order to serve science" (7). In other words, the present age has deliberately weakened or dried up its passion for the sake of book-learning. People "live in their thoughts," not in the old-fashioned way of acting with passion. Since admiration and horror are passions, the present age is ill-equipped to admire faith as it deserves, and to feel the appropriate horror at the courage which enables it to make dreadful sacrifices. Silentio also suggests that his age is dominated by "bourgeoise philistinism," which another of Kierkegaard's pseudonyms defines as a lack of *imagination* (FT 61; SUD 41). But deficiency in imagination makes it difficult to admire faith or to feel horror at it. Silentio says that people believe they know that faith is something easy and trivial, but in fact they do not understand faith, because they think about it by way of *cliches* (FT 55). Another problem is that people *think inhumanly* about Christ and faith in him (64–66). The knight of faith Abraham lived long ago and far away, so that he may not seem to be a human being like us, whose life is relevant to ours, and whom we might imitate. Moreover, we know the happy ending of his trial and its effect upon history, and we think about the *result* of his trial, not about his experience as he was tested by God. But to think about the result, and not about the experience of the test, is to think inhumanly about faith.

Since Silentio believes that his readers are in many ways unwilling and unable to admire faith and feel horrified by it, he must do more than merely praise it. He must also train people to appreciate his praise. In order to train and exercise his readers, Silentio artfully shocks, disturbs, and disorients them, and employs clever scare tactics on them, in order to evoke fear, terror, and anxiety, and thus awaken their passion.

He is also a model of relating rightly to Abraham, with passion, horror, honesty, and personal concern. He constantly expresses his admiration of, and horror at, Abraham's deeds of faith; and he frequently confesses his inferiority to the knight of faith with honesty and humility. He walks us through how he thinks humanly about Abraham, and how he applies Abraham's trial of faith to himself with concern. And because he seems credible, we tend to imitate his relation to Abraham and to the knight of faith. Thus he is much more than a poet. He is also a model, a nonviolent terrorist, a therapist, and a trainer. In fact he thinks that the problem of praising faith to a readership which is unreceptive to his praise is so difficult that he must also be a spy and a deceiver in the service of truth. But that is not a topic for this introduction to Kierkegaard.

In the first chapter of *Fear and Trembling* Silentio "tunes up" his readers' imagination. He tells a story about a man whose "one wish" and "one longing" was to "see Abraham," "to have witnessed that event" of his trial, and "to be present in that hour when Abraham raised his eyes and saw Mount Moriah in the distance" (9). This man is a model for us to imitate of concerned and imaginative thinking about faith. Silentio describes four ways that this unnamed person tells himself the story of the trial of

Abraham. Remarkably, if we compare these four versions of Abraham's story to the way Silentio himself tells it, they contain many errors and misunderstandings. Why then would Silentio present his readers with seriously defective stories of Abraham? It is because he wishes to *attune* them to their task, by helping them practice thinking in the right spirit about the faith of Abraham. Most generally, he trains one's imagination, making it stronger, more passionate, more flexible, and more sensitive.

After tuning up and training his reader's imagination and passion, Silentio proceeds in the next chapter to retell the story of Abraham. What *Genesis* tells us about Abraham is quite sparse, since it describes virtually nothing about what Abraham thought or felt when he was tested by God. But a person who is "made sleepless" by the trial of the father of faith would be eagerly concerned to know what this trial meant to the one who endured it and triumphed in it. Therefore Silentio imagines the inner life of Abraham, giving verve and pathos to the story, thereby making it new and exciting. In order to help us imaginatively appreciate the greatness of Abraham, Silentio invents the striking figure of the "knight of faith," and transplants knights of faith into traditional stories, thus fruitfully blending the strange and the familiar. Silentio adapts many myths and legends so that they either contain an illuminating analogue to faith, or something instructively different from Abraham's story. The most important instructive difference from faith is to be found in the demonic individual, who is so strong and courageous that he becomes deeply aware of the possibility of offense, and cannot then turn back to living a middling sort of life, but must either embrace faith, or else stand firm in defiance of the divine command to obey and pray for help. It is hard to hold on to a superficial misunderstanding of faith by way of cliches when we see it uncannily reimagined and set down in unfamiliar territory.

In one striking paragraph Silentio turns his imagination to the project of putting himself in the place of someone contemporary with Christ (66). In doing so he intimates the strangeness, fearfulness, and difficulty of encountering Christ in person, but also the exhilaration of it. As we shall see in a later chapter, the most important thing in becoming a Christian, according to Kierkegaard, is to become contemporary in imagination with Christ. Silentio devotes only one paragraph to this task, so that what he provides us is only a sketch, which hints at a future challenge for readers, and begins to attune them to it.

One of the most potent versions of a knight of faith in *Fear and Trembling* is a contemporary one who "looks just like a tax collector" (39).

Silentio stresses the seeming ordinariness of the man, and the unrecognizability of his excellence. Silentio does this in order to stress that faith exists in the soul of the believer, not in external deeds, and to stress that faith is possible for all people in all situations. He also emphasizes that in order to be a knight of faith one must be a single individual who takes responsibility for his or her life. Silentio even claims that the "dreadfulness of faith" is to be a single individual who says "You" to God in heaven (77). It is worth pondering how being a solitary self, alone before God, is as terrible and dreadful as being tried by God with a command to sacrifice a loved one. Great passion and imagination would be required to perceive this dreadfulness adequately.

Another function of imagination is to make people aware of possibility. Perhaps people have trouble believing that a knight of faith is possible at all, and great difficulty in believing in this possibility for themselves. According to another pseudonym of Kierkegaard, Anti-Climacus, it is by imagination that people become profoundly aware of possibility, especially the existential possibility of imitating sublime ideals like that of the knight of faith (SUD 39, 41). Thus an important function of Silentio's imaginative poetry is to help readers to become aware of their tremendous potential as human beings.

In the previous chapters about A and Judge William, we considered the defects and limitations of these two persons and of their lives. We have also already criticized Silentio insofar as he is a knight of infinite resignation. Let us now criticize him a little in his capacity as a poet. As a poet Silentio helpfully models ways of relating rightly to Abraham and his faith. But his poetic existence also has flaws. He repeatedly says that he "cannot make the movement of faith" (FT 36). If you search his book for explanations of his incapacity, you will find exceedingly few, and lame ones at that, which Kierkegaard himself elsewhere devastatingly criticizes, but without mentioning Silentio. Tellingly, Silentio never says that he attempts to make the movement of faith. Perhaps he is not especially eager to try. And yet, according to Silentio, "no human being is excluded from" faith, and "true greatness is equally accessible to all" people (67; 81). But if all people can have faith, then so can Silentio, unless he were to ingeniously excuse himself on the grounds that he is a fictitious persona created by Kierkegaard merely to praise faith, not to have it. So we see that Silentio could have faith, but does not have it, and does not even strive for it. Furthermore, he claims that the poet is "happy" that the hero whom he admires is "not himself, that his love can be admiration" (FT 15). This implies that Silentio is happy merely to admire and praise Abraham, without attempting to imitate him.

Given that Silentio is content to be a poet of faith, and not a knight of faith, he must have vices that prevent him from striving to be what he most admires and celebrates as the "greatest of all." But his vices are only part of the story. Another part is the sublime power of his poetry. Describing the virtue of imagination, which creates poetry, Kierkegaard writes the following: "Imagination is what providence uses to take men captive in actuality, in existence, in order to get them far enough out, or within, or down into actuality. And when imagination has helped them to get as far out as they should be—then actuality genuinely begins" (JP 2 1832). God gives imagination to people to lure them towards heroic life in service of ideals. It is because they have such potent imaginations that human beings can write and be moved by poetry that praises ideals like that of faith. If imagination and the poetry it creates were not sublime, then human beings could not be lured into heroic endeavors. But, because poetry is potent and enchanting, it is possible to make an idol of it. Silentio is a great idolater of poetry. God lays bait in the form of poetry to trap people in the task of heroic striving, and like a fox Silentio steals the bait while cunningly avoiding the trap.

In making a jest about the present state of philosophy at his time, David Hume says that the "victory is not gained by the men at arms, who manage the pike and the sword; but by the trumpeters, drummers, and musicians of the army."[1] Of course Hume intends to mock a martial struggle won not by warriors but by artists, but we could also marvel that the trumpeters, drummers, and musicians of the army can accomplish so much. The reason that they can achieve victory is the power of imagination that creates poetry as well as music. Silentio wins a victory with his poetry, and is content with that. In a fit of enthusiasm, while addressing and eulogizing Abraham, Silentio evens says that "you reward your lover more gloriously than anyone else. In the life to come you make him eternally happy in your bosom; here in this life you captivate his eyes and his heart with the wonder of your act" (23). This seems a bit immodest. Abraham endured the most terrible trial. How then could a admirer of him such as Silentio be rewarded equally with the great patriarch and father of faith?[2]

---

1. Hume, *Treatise*, 41–42.
2. For a fuller account of how Kierkegaard praises faith, and uses Silentio to praise it, see McCombs, *Art and Praise*, 23–50.

CHAPTER FIVE

The Most Interesting Man Who Ever Lived

KIERKEGAARD PRAISES HEROISM BECAUSE he believes that there are causes worth championing, and that it is possible to champion them admirably. He also thinks that other causes deserve to be attacked, and he is almost always on the attack against someone or something, be it a newspaper, a philosopher, or the modern age in Western Europe. Hegelian philosophy especially provokes his ire, because he thinks it dishonestly distorts Christianity in order to coopt it for humanistic purposes. He also thinks Hegelians are idolatrously fascinated with history and politics, with the result that they neglect issues of the greatest importance, especially the ethical and religious development of individual human beings. If individuals have eternal souls and will face divine judgment, but states are merely temporal, then the Hegelians are perniciously wrong to elevate politics above ethics and religion. Such soul-destroying teaching does not call for polite or demure objections, but a heroic attack.

Kierkegaard wages war against Hegelian philosophy so passionately that he gives many readers the impression that he rejects the philosophical ideals of reason and knowledge in order to affirm faith. If this common opinion about him were correct, we would expect him to disapprove of philosophers and thinkers. But in fact he enthusiastically admires and praises several intellectual heroes, and adapts their thought to his religious purposes.

The Most Interesting Man Who Ever Lived

It is difficult to praise a heroic thinker, or to tell his story engagingly, for the general public. An indication of this difficulty is that Hollywood makes no movies about the drama of great thinking. Film never or rarely attempts to reveal the heroism and adventure of thought. In nearly all films about intellectual heroes, the drama comes from somewhere other than the quest for truth or artistic beauty. The interest derives instead from the hero's struggle with trauma, mental illness, or drug addiction. The most marketable kind of thinker in film today is the detective. Nearly all recent TV shows and novels about detectives stress the psychological wounds or suffering of the protagonist.

Kierkegaard's praise of intellectual heroes such as Lessing and Luther is remarkably inspiring, and one of his books movingly describes the growth of a heroic thinker, named Johannes Climacus, who is the pseudonymous author of two other books of Kierkegaard. This biography tells the story of how its hero strives to enter into an authentic personal relation to doubt, and discovers in doubt "the beginning of the highest form of existence" (JC 170).

The hero of thought whom Kierkegaard most ardently admires is "that simple wise man of old," namely, Socrates. The figure of Socrates is ubiquitous in Kierkegaard's authorship, where he towers over every other hero, except perhaps Abraham, whom Kierkegaard highly fictionalizes, and whom he talks about at length only in one book, and of course Christ, who is much more than a hero. Kierkegaard calls Socrates "the greatest hero" of Greece, and "the most interesting man who ever lived" (CUP 368; FT 83).

Many heroes are not especially interesting, and many an interesting fellow is utterly unheroic. But Socrates is supremely heroic and superlatively interesting, and there is a profound connection between his noble courageousness and his fascinating mysteriousness. Johannes de Silentio writes that Socrates had to *acquire* his interesting *existence* with "trouble and pain" (FT 83). In other words, Socrates became interesting through heroic struggle. Our task in this present chapter is to see how he did this. For now I will observe that Socrates, as understood by Kierkegaard, hid his heroism in order to express reverence for the god, and so as not to crush the spirit of other people, whom he wished to build up to become the heroes of their own lives. To struggle heroically, and then not to take credit for one's struggle, is itself a difficult task requiring heroic effort. But Socrates did not completely conceal his heroism. As we shall see, he also found it necessary partly to reveal his own greatness in order to achieve his ethical and religious purposes. By partly concealing and partly revealing his heroic struggle Socrates created the most interesting tension that, according to Kierkegaard, a human being has ever created.

Kierkegaard's preference for Socrates over all other heroes is strange, almost inexplicable. Since Kierkegaard professes to have faith in Christ, we would have expected him to rank a Christian hero or saint higher than Socrates. But he does not. Since he thinks that becoming a Christian means being remade by divine omnipotence, why do no divinely regenerated Christians garner more of Kierkegaard's praise and admiration than the unregenerate Socrates does? Given Kierkegaard's belief that Christian revelation teaches human beings truths that they could not learn by their own unaided efforts, why does he say that Socrates is the "only *man* I admiringly recognize as teacher," even though Socrates was not a recipient of Christian revelation (AUP 283)? It is especially striking and strange that Kierkegaard greatly admires Luther and Socrates, but Socrates affirms reason as divine, and Luther calls it *Satan* and a *whore*. It is as if Kierkegaard's two favorite political heroes were Alexander the Great and Mahatma Gandhi.

In this chapter we will examine the figure of Socrates, not just in one of Kierkegaard's books, but throughout his writings. We will see why Kierkegaard admires Socrates, and I will try to give you a sense of Kierkegaard's appropriation of many aspects of Socratic thought for Christian use: Socrates's honesty, courage, and rigor in thinking, his distinction-making, his self-examination in quest of self-knowledge, his focus on ethical inquiry, his famous profession of ignorance, his erotic longing for the divine, his irony, his artful synthesis of playfulness and seriousness, and his theory and practice of pedagogy. I will end the chapter by showing that Kierkegaard treats Socrates as a sort of pagan prophet of Christ, thereby suggesting that the "merely human" has a sort of goodness deep within it that helps a virtuous pagan to welcome the "essentially Christian" when it arrives.

Even though Socrates was a genius, Kierkegaard praises him much more for his virtue than for his brilliance. He eulogizes Socrates because he is ethically serious, honest, courageous, generous towards other learners, humble, and simple. The simplicity of Socrates consists partly in putting his thoughts into practice so thoroughly and naturally that he "artistically exemplified what he had understood" (PF 10). Another aspect of his simplicity is that he talks plainly and unpretentiously to common people in the *marketplace* (11). Being simple means being one and undivided. Because there is no division between what Socrates understands and what he does in his life, and no division between him an ordinary people, he deserves to be called "that simple wise man of old."

Kierkegaard praises Socrates for making "absolute distinctions," and blames the Hegelians for blurring and fudging conflicting categories instead of strictly distinguishing them from one another (108). This praise and blame might seem to suggest that Kierkegaard values intellectual rigor for its own sake. But in fact he values utterly clear either/ors because heroism requires them. In order to be heroically dedicated to an ideal, by living for it consistently and without compromise, one must be clear what it requires, and not confuse it with other ideals. Therefore, Kierkegaard's concern for absolute distinctions is not pedantically intellectual but earnestly ethical and religious. He thinks that the Hegelians confuse different ways of life to avoid heroically choosing one definite course of action with all its costs and sacrifices. For if you choose this way of life, and reject that one, then you must also reject many of the pleasures and comforts of that one. But the Hegelians do not want to make painful sacrifices. To avoid making them, and to try to have it all, they confusingly blur the boundaries between different ways of life. It is as though they thought they could lie in bed until noon every day, and then feast on cake and ice cream, but also be fierce and formidable warriors. Kierkegaard is especially indignant that the Hegelians pretend to combine Christianity and their unethical style of philosophizing without compromising either of them, and his book *Philosophical Fragments* is dedicated to using Socratic dialectic or logic to distinguish between Christianity and merely human philosophy.

Kierkegaard's conception of intellectual heroism is aptly symbolized in the first story of the most famous intellectual hero of modern fiction. When Dr. Watson is introduced to Sherlock Holmes, almost the first thing that comes to light about Holmes is that he is not aware of the Copernican theory that the earth goes round the sun. Watson then expresses amazement that Holmes does not know this simple fact that every schoolchild knows, and the latter replies that since such knowledge will not help him to become a great detective—which is all he cares about—he will now do his best to forget this irrelevant astronomical information so that he can dedicate himself wholly to crime-solving. It was brilliant of Sir Arthur Conan Doyle to introduce his hero to us by showing the detective's single-minded devotion to his vocation. Even though Kierkegaard would not think as highly of detective work as Holmes does, he would, I believe, praise the sleuth's heroic dedication to his noble task, and he might also see in crime investigation an image of a greater tasks, namely, ethical self-examination and prophetic denunciation of the evils of the age. For ethical self-examination, prophecy, and crime-solving are concerned with the discovery of evil—and sometimes of good—but for different purposes and in different contexts.

Probably the most famous statement about self-examination in the history of the West is that of Socrates, who said that the "unexamined life is not worth living,"[1] and who was unstinting in his examination of his own life and in helping others to examine theirs. When Phaedrus asks him whether he believes a certain famous Athenian myth, Socrates responds that he does not have time to inquire into such things as long as he does not *know himself,* "whether he is a wild beast more tangled and puffed up with pride than Typhon," who is an enemy of the gods, "or a gentler and simpler creature who is akin to the divine."[2] These words artfully express, in maximally compressed form, almost the whole purpose of self-examination as it is understood by Kierkegaard. Socrates asks ethical and religious questions about himself: is he proud, is he an enemy of the gods, or he is akin to the divine and friendly towards it. Socrates investigates himself in particular and human nature in general (his question whether he is akin to the divine is about human nature). Kierkegaard praises him for the results of his heroic efforts at self-examination: "not many have lived who knew human nature as well as Socrates did, who in addition knew himself" (PV 141). Both for Socrates and Kierkegaard, ethical self-examination is directed by three fundamental questions: what are my most sincere ethical beliefs, are they consistent with one another, and does my life faithfully express these convictions.

Kierkegaard wholly approves of the Socratic quest for self-knowledge at the expense of nearly all other forms of learning. It is almost as if he said that the only allowable inquiry is self-examination. But, he adds, one may or should also inquire into other things that have a bearing on or assist self-examination, like the greatest tragedies, epics, and novels. This proviso may considerably expand the range of permissible inquiry. Finally, he concedes that since we are weak and often in need of refreshment, we may turn to less serious studies, if we really use them for rejuvenation, and not to evade the task of fulfilling our duties. Kierkegaard starkly contrasts the devotion of Socrates to self-examination with the Hegelian mentality, which is the exact

1. Plato, *Apology,* 38a.
2. Plato, *Phaedrus,* 230a.

opposite of the Socratic, in that it neglects self-knowledge in its search for speculative understanding of metaphysics, history, and politics. Because Hegelian thinking shirks the pursuit of self-knowledge, Kierkegaard calls it *unethical* and *fantastic*. Instead of focusing on the most important reality for a person, namely, his or her own spiritual condition, it wastes time pursuing hard to acquire and irrelevant speculative knowledge.

Self-examination is a risky endeavor requiring heroic courage. It involves facing up to frightening possibilities about oneself, and a willingness to discover one's faults, vices, sins, and guilt. Through it one may also discover painful and arduous duties. Besides examining himself, Socrates helped, encouraged, and almost forced his fellow citizens to examine themselves, and they often were quite unappreciative of the unflattering self-awareness that this examination produced. People may sometimes admire and praise a truth-speaker when he pulls his punches and tells the truth only "to a certain degree." But if a person speaks the truth uncompromisingly, and at the expense of other people's vanity, he becomes odious to them, and puts himself in great peril, if the others have any significant power over him. Since Socrates was not naïve, he knew well that his cross-examination of other people made many of them extremely angry with him, and that these enraged people might consequently get their revenge on him or even put him to death, as they in fact eventually did. Given that Socrates publicly pursued the truth in full knowledge of the dangers, refused to yield to the enemies of truth when they threatened him with dire consequences, and then nobly endured his trial, death-sentence, and execution, Kierkegaard calls him the "only true martyr of intellectuality" (TM 341).

Kierkegaard imitated Socrates by assisting his readers to know themselves, sometimes in a cooperative spirit, as he does in *For Self-Examination* and *Judge For Yourselves*, and sometimes in a polemical spirit, as in the *Attack Upon Christendom*. Therefore reading him is nearly always a tutorial in self-examination, and sometimes the occasion for surprising and unwelcome realizations about oneself.

Although Socrates sought to know himself and helped others do likewise, his irony made it difficult for other people to know him. Irony is conventionally conceived as condescending insincerity, whose purpose is to imply one's superiority over others, or to play elusively with them instead of taking them seriously. Socratic irony is also playful, elusive, and sometimes insincere. Sometimes Socrates says things as if he were serious when in fact he is jesting, and sometimes he says things as if he were jesting when in fact he is serious. This second aspect of Socratic irony is not generally appreciated as much as the first is, but, Kierkegaard thinks, it is just as important. Socratic irony differs from the conventional sort in that it is not an assertion of one's superiority, but expresses essential human equality, and in that it does not trifle with others, but is a way of taking them most seriously. Through his irony Socrates avoids being an authority for others—for authority tends to erode human dignity and responsibility—and provokes people to think and act for themselves. Besides the danger that by teaching people Socrates will tempt them to treat him abjectly as an authority, there is the converse danger that learners could become authorities for him. This second danger is not as obvious as the first, so that a word about it is in order. It is tempting for a teacher who enjoys the admiration of students to develop a need to be admired, and then to compromise his message and methods in order to win admiration. If he succumbs to this temptation, then he had made his students unhealthily dependent on him, and himself unhealthily dependent on them. Socrates employs irony as a means of repelling potential groupies. Through his irony he carves out for himself (and invites others to carve out for themselves) an independent interior reality, which Kierkegaard thinks is an essential part of personhood and sometimes calls "hidden inwardness."

Socratic irony involves a mixture of seriousness and jest.[3] He is serious because he seeks truth and goodness, which are ideals of great worth. He is playful because he is aware that he and others are tempted to treat him and his pedagogical assistance as more important and potent than they really are. As a remedy to this temptation, Socrates puts a hint of jest and playfulness into his words and manner, even as he also expresses serious reverence for the ideals. It is not enough, however, to be both serious and playful. One must artfully combine them in the right way. Kierkegaard thinks that Socrates talks with a brilliantly artful combination of seriousness and jest, and imitates this combination in his own writing.

It is easy to overestimate the extent to which Socrates ironically conceals his message, and to misunderstand his purpose in concealing it. Socrates is to be sure enigmatic, but he is not completely mystifying. What is more, he conceals his teaching in order the better to reveal it. By concealing it, but with apt and skillful hints sprinkled in here and there, he provokes learners to discover truth for themselves. He points them in the right direction, and then leaves them free to seek and find for themselves.

3. Plato, *Phaedrus*, 276d, 277e.

Sometimes people are mystifying in order to feel superior to others, or to manipulate them. But Socrates is enigmatic to establish equality with others. He thinks that all people without distinction must discover ethical and religious truths within themselves and for themselves. Only when *you* discover an existential truth is it discovered *for you*. You must listen to your own conscience to know what it says. It would be a contradiction in terms for another person to speak for your conscience. Another person cannot be responsible for you on your behalf. Understanding all this thoroughly, Socrates is ironic in order to encourage people to become self-active, conscientious, and responsible for themselves in their search for truth and virtue. Irony, therefore, is not for him an optional pedagogical technique, but the essential means for helping others to live as they are called to.

Let us recall that the esthete named "A" idolized the interesting, and that the interesting consists partly in a tension between concealment and revelation. Let us also remember that Judge William argued that ethically respecting other people makes them more interesting, because it leaves them free to surprise us when they express the tension between their appearance and their reality. Socrates renders human life even more interesting than Judge William through his practice of irony, which promotes hidden and substantial inwardness in himself and in other people. Socratic irony and hidden inwardness heighten the tension between concealment and revelation in human beings' ethical relations with one another. Since Socrates was not only the master of irony, but helped others to acquire this interesting art, he is according to Silentio the "most interesting man who ever lived" (FT 83). And since he is immensely interested in the service of ethics, he succeeds more than Judge William at synthesizing the esthetic with the ethical.

Socrates's irony is closely connected to his famous profession of ignorance. Kierkegaard's pseudonym Johannes Climacus interprets Socrates's ignorance as ironic when he says that this ignorance is a "unitive expression of love for the learner" (PF 30). In other words, out of love Socrates pretends to be as ignorant as his interlocutor, so that he may unite himself to him and share inquiry with him.

This is not to say, however, that Socrates is always insincere when he stresses the limits of his knowledge. For these limits have a profound religious significance, and becoming aware of them is a heroic task. You will recall that Silentio defines the heroic movement of infinite resignation as passionate awareness of the limits of one's abilities and of the precariousness of one's seeming possessions. The first part of this definition describes Socratic ignorance, so that it is not surprising that Silentio mentions the "Socratic... movement of ignorance" as an example of infinite resignation (FT 42). We might even hypothesize that Socratic ignorance is Kierkegaard's inspiration for his conception of the knight of infinite resignation.

Anti-Climacus, who is another of Kierkegaard's pseudonyms, writes the following about Socratic ignorance: "let us never forget that it was out of reverence for God that [Socrates] was ignorant, that as far as it was possible for a pagan he was on guard duty as a judge on the frontier between God and man, keeping watch so that the deep gulf of qualitative difference between... God and man... was maintained" (SUD 99). This passage is in part an interpretation of the *Apology*, where Socrates claims it is in "service of the god" that he questions people and exposes their pretensions to knowledge.[4] A sophisticated reader might suspect that Socrates jests when he claims that by cross-examining people he is serving the god. After all, Socrates admits that he enjoys refuting people, and he might have found it amusing to justify his fun at other people's expense by calling it divine service. No doubt Kierkegaard would acknowledge that Socrates seems to be jesting when he calls his practice of exposing pretentious ignorance a kind of worship. But I think he would one-up the sophisticated reader by suggesting that Socrates's jesting appearance is ironic, so that Socrates really is serious when he claims to be serving the god by cross-examining his fellow citizens. Socrates asserts at the beginning of his self-defense in the *Apology* that he will tell the "whole truth," and Kierkegaard cunningly takes him at his word.[5]

When Anti-Climacus writes that it was out of reverence for God that Socrates was ignorant, he suggests that Socrates was not totally ignorant, and that he claimed to be ignorant in order to express reverence for God. This suggestion is confirmed when Anti-Climacus says that Socrates was on guard duty as a judge at the frontier between God and man. If Socrates is qualified to be a judge at the border between the divine and the human, then he must understand that God deserves reverence, how to detect immodest speech about God, and how to use a profession of ignorance as an expression of reverence. Therefore his ignorance is a knowledgeable ignorance, a paradoxical ignorance in which there is an intimation of divine, transcendent reality.

4. Plato, *Apology*, 23c.
5. Plato, *Apology*, 17b.

It is tempting to profess Socratic ignorance to avoid strenuous efforts to understand things that one could and ought to understand. But such shirking is not faithful imitation of Socrates, who was always seeking to understand important things, and urging others to do the same. Strictly speaking, Socratic ignorance is an awareness that one does not *yet* understand this or that, not an awareness that one could *never* understand it or make progress in understanding it. Socrates never says he *knows that he cannot know* something, and famously criticizes skepticism in the *Phaedo*. When I become Socratically aware that I do not yet understand something vital or serious, this awareness should be a goad to further inquiry, not an excuse to be lazy and complacent.

A large part of the Socratic remedy to skeptical laziness is *eros*, which urges a discouraged seeker onward. In the *Phaedrus* and the *Symposium* Socrates propounds the theory that sexual desire, or eros, aims at more than intercourse. Eros as understood by Socrates is a desire for divine beauty, goodness, and wisdom. Socrates connects sex with yearnings for the divine partly because he notices that people in love see a divine significance in the beloved and are therefore willing to make great sacrifices for her as if she were a deity. Socrates infers from these phenomena that sexual desire contains a longing for divine things, with the beloved as a symbol of the deity. It is therefore easy to understand how Socratic eros is a complement to Socratic ignorance. If you are discouraged when you become aware of your ignorance, eros can inspire you to seek the knowledge that you lack.

As Kierkegaard adapts Socratic distinction-making, irony, and ignorance to his own purposes, so also he adapts eros. In *Philosophical Fragments* his pseudonym, Johannes Climacus, rechristens Socratic eros as the "passion of thought," and describes it as restlessly searching for what transcends human cognition (PF 37). This passion of thought does not crave mere mystery, or nonsense, but whatever is greatest, most wonderful, and most sublime. As Climacus sees it, the reality that best answers to and satisfies the passion of thought is the incarnation of God as a human being.

Perhaps the most important thing for Kierkegaard about Socrates is that he strives to "stand alone" and to help other people to do the same thing. To stand alone means to be "free, independent, [one's] own master," and a "distinct individuality" (274, 272). In short, it means being a hero. If you stand alone, then just by that fact you are a *self*, and have fulfilled an essential requirement of the human vocation. In his writing Kierkegaard attempts to help readers becomes selves, partly by addressing them earnestly as single individuals. He writes that if you can get people alone and separated from the human crowd, there is ever so much good in them (PV 11). When people are really alone in their interior castles, they become ready to encounter God, who may then reveal himself to them or otherwise help them. Human beings put other people between themselves and God to avoid the fearful divine encounter with its strenuousness and terrible responsibility, so that when one stops using other people as screens between oneself and God, a revelation may occur. You can see, therefore, why Kierkegaard says that to help another person to stand alone is "the greatest beneficence" (WL 274).

According to Kierkegaard, it is immensely difficult to help other people to stand solo. For becoming an independent self is laborious and involves frightening responsibility. Therefore, we often stubbornly resist a Socratic teacher's efforts to help us stand alone. This resistance can be quite devious. Even when you seem to be willing to stand alone and apart from your Socratic teacher, there is the danger that your gratitude will make you dependent on him. It is crucial, therefore, to remember that a human teacher cannot give you anything essential, and that your own efforts are the key to your learning and growth. Since gratitude can make people forget this essential truth, it is necessary for Socratic teachers to emphasize the efforts of their students, and to downplay and even hide their own contributions to their students' growth. Because of the necessity of this concealment, Kierkegaard says that the Socratic teacher *deceives* people "into the truth" (WL 277). Socrates, Kierkegaard claims, is the supreme artist of using deception to enlighten others. The strangeness in the idea of deceiving someone into the truth matches well the paradox involved in helping another person to stand alone. How can you be a prop, even a vanishing prop, by which another person stands unassisted on his own two feet? We might also note that the notion of deceiving people into the truth is immensely interesting.

Helpful deception requires more than artistry. To be a Socratic pedagogue requires self-denial, humility, and love. Socrates needs great love for other learners in order to take so much trouble to help them, knowing that many of them will not thank him for his assistance, but may even wish him harm in return for his love. He requires self-denying humility so as not to take credit for the help that he gives people, and even to hide his assistance. Kierkegaard praises the loving humility of Socrates when he says that the latter was only an *occasion* of learning "even for the most stupid person" (PF 11). It is ever so tempting to give answers to sluggish learners. But, according to Kierkegaard, Socrates had the patience and love to allow even the most dull-witted person to learn for himself.

Much in Kierkegaard's authorship is an attempt to do for his readers the "greatest beneficence" of helping them to become independent selves; and in his efforts to do this good deed he imitates Socratic pedagogy. Kierkegaard's elusive style, which makes readers work for what they learn, his use of irony and of pseudonyms, by which he avoids becoming an authority for his readers, his efforts to deceive people into the truth, by which he hides his assistance and keeps the stress on the efforts of those being assisted, and his attempt to meet his readers where they are in order to lead them to where he wants them to go, as Socrates worked with the assumptions of his interlocutors, are all imitations of Socratic pedagogy. Kierkegaard's common name for these various pedagogical tactics is "indirect communication," which he employs throughout his authorship, but more extensively in his pseudonymous writings, which we have been focusing on in this book.

Perhaps the most interesting thing, and certainly the most mysterious thing, about Socrates is that he claims to be visited by a *daemon*, or *daimonion*, which seems to be a minor divinity, or a sort of tutelary spirit. Socrates says that his daemon comes to him from time to time and tells him not to do something that he was about to do.[6] It is therefore a sort of negative guide or teacher. As Socrates's ignorance vetoes his opinion that he knows this or that, his daemon vetoes this or that action that Socrates proposes to himself to perform. Probably most sophisticated readers of Plato regard Socrates's talk about his daemon as jesting or ironic. It amuses them to think that Socrates justifies his unconventional behavior by claiming to be religiously inspired. Kierkegaard, however, detects a deeper irony: although Socrates seems to sophisticated readers to be jesting about his daemon, in fact he is serious, and the joke is on them.

If Kierkegaard is right and Socrates is sincere about his ever so private spiritual counselor, then Socrates claims that a divinity helps him to transcend merely human wisdom. As we have seen, transcendence is a common theme in Socratic ignorance, Socratic eros, and Socratic pedagogy. Socratic ignorance transcends itself in prophetic intimations of some great truth. Socratic eros has an instinct that detects its own downfall in what transcends thought. Socratic pedagogy aims to put a person alone before God, to be taught and helped by God. The name of the most Socratic of Kierkegaard's pseudonyms also suggests transcendence, namely, *Johannes*

---

6. Plato, *Apology*, 40a–b.

Climacus, which means something like John of the Ladder. Kierkegaard says in a biography which he wrote about this fictitious author that Climacus regards "coherent thinking" as a *ladder* for climbing to *paradise* (JC 118). In his name and in many of his ideas Climacus is an apt symbol of the human capacity for transcendence.

Although the human ability to transcend limits is a major theme in Kierkegaard's writings, he does not talk much about it directly. Instead, he suggests it, and his hints of transcendence pervade his whole authorship. The clues work something like this: over and over Kierkegaard declares limits to human nature, but then implies that these limits can be surpassed. Like Socrates, he stands on guard duty at the border between the divine and the human so that he may chastise proud and excessive ambition. Stationed at his post, he exposes vain human pretensions, and says sternly, "None may pass." He is especially severe with Hegelian thinkers for their empty boasts to "go further" than natural human limits. It is quite puzzling, therefore, that Kierkegaard himself declares human limits, and then sometimes implies that Socrates or someone else transcends them. We will consider several examples.

In *Philosophical Fragments* the chief task is to distinguish Christianity from the best merely human philosophy, namely, that of Socrates. Besides making this distinction, the book also says that Socrates is "forever right" about how to help people learn the truth, even Christian truth (PF 10). It is quite strange that a pagan discovered the best way to teach revealed Christian truth. How can Socrates divine so well the right way to talk about Jesus?

In *Philosophical Fragments* Johannes Climacus says that without Christian revelation a human being cannot "even be a seeker," but is an enemy of Christian truth (13, 15). But he also says that "the passion of thought," which is always present in all human thought, though often only implicitly, desires to "discover that which thought itself cannot think," namely, the absolute paradox that God became incarnate in the person of Jesus Christ (PF 37; see also 38–48). In short, all people, says Climacus, even without revelation, desire Jesus Christ in all their thoughts, but usually without knowing it. How strange that human beings cannot even seek the truth without Christian revelation, but also desire in all their thinking the greatest Christian truth, the truth incarnate in Jesus Christ.

Again, in *Philosophical Fragments*, Climacus claims that no human being can discover without Christian revelation that he or she is a sinner

(47). But, in a passage that we have already considered, Climacus quotes the part of the *Phaedrus* where Socrates says he suspects that he may be puffed up with pride and an enemy of the gods, like the monster Typhon (39; cf. SUD 116). This quotation seems to say that Socrates had intimations that he was a sinner. To be sure, Climacus does not assert that Socrates discovered he was a sinner, but only suggests that Socrates had his suspicions. If Socrates does not quite transcend the limit set for him by Climacus, he at least encroaches upon it, and threatens to surpass it.

In *Works of Love* Kierkegaard claims that no human being can discover the Christian teaching about loving one's neighbor as oneself. But he also describes Socrates as coming very close to loving people as Christ commanded. For example, he says that both Socrates and Christian love help other people to stand alone (WL 276–77). Then he says that Socrates was not as deeply *concerned* to help other people as Christian charity is concerned to help (277). That is a small difference, and Socratic love is at a minimum quite prophetic of Christian love.

Consider the following hierarchy propounded by Kierkegaard: there is, he says, "the highest degree of self-love that the world . . . calls self-love; the self-love of the alliance [that] the world calls love; a noble, self-sacrificing, magnanimous, human love [namely, that of Socrates] that still is not Christian love [but that] is ridiculed by the world as foolishness;" and "Christian love [which] is hated, detested, and persecuted by the world as foolishness" (120). In this hierarchy Socrates comes remarkably close to Christian love. Kierkegaard refers to a passage in Plato in which Socrates jests about *loving the ugly*, and comments that "the ugly is the neighbor," because just as one does not love one's neighbor as oneself by inclination, but in obedience to a divine command, so one does not love the ugly by inclination. Kierkegaard goes on to say that when Socrates spoke of loving the ugly he was "only teasing" or playing. Probably he was, but Kierkegaard goes out of his way to show that the jest of Socrates prophetically anticipates Christian love (373–74).

Kierkegaard writes that Socrates is the inventor of the *category* of the "single individual," and that he was the only person to use this category before the advent of Christianity. Kierkegaard also says that "this category" will be used now "to make people . . . Christians." Moreover, he is astonishingly confident in the power of this category: "One can promise to make a Christian of every individual one can get under this category [of the single individual]—insofar as one person can do this for another." The "single individual" who "is alone . . . before God . . . will no doubt manage to obey" (PV 123). This is to say that Socrates invented a most potent evangelical category. How amazing that Socrates could proselytize for Christianity so well when he knew nothing of the Gospel!

Kierkegaard writes that he is "definitely . . . convinced that" Socrates "has become" a Christian (54). If Socrates was bound to become a Christian, this implies that human nature finds its fulfillment in Christianity, and that through heroic striving for wisdom and virtue a mere human being can, unawares, become ready to welcome Christian revelation when it comes—even if he is dead at its advent.

It is hard to stress adequately the strangeness of Kierkegaard's attributing to Socrates a daemonic power to prophecy about Christ and to prepare the way of the Lord. In order to appreciate the strangeness of it, you would have to read hundreds of passages in which Kierkegaard insists on keeping Christianity distinct from "the merely human." And you would also have to see that he repeatedly speaks about reason and knowledge in a way which suggests that he rejects or disrespects them. Then you would be properly prepared to be astonished by the almost Christian wisdom that Kierkegaard attributes to the pagan philosopher who loved reason so much that he professed to follow the argument wherever it leads.

A qualification is in order here. Kierkegaard sets limits and then implies that Socrates encroaches on some of them and surpasses others. But Kierkegaard carefully keeps Socrates within some crucial limits. He does not represent Socrates as pre-inventing Christianity. He does not say Socrates prophesied the incarnation of the creator of the world. He does not claim that Socrates on his own defines sin correctly, or that he saves himself from sin without divine aid.

What then is the meaning of Kierkegaard's practice of declaring natural human limits and then suggesting that Socrates surpasses some of them? Is Kierkegaard confused? Does he love Christianity and Socrates, but get into a muddle when he tries to stay true to each of these perhaps incompatible loves? Honestly, to me that seems impossible. I think Kierkegaard must know what he is doing. But what exactly is he up to in making Socrates a sort of pagan prophet of Christ? Two things, I think. First, he wants to stress that Christianity fulfills and perfects human nature. He presents Socrates as an image of humanity at its best without Christian revelation, and then describes Socrates making the kind of progress towards Christianity that unaided human nature can make. Second, I think Kierkegaard wants to use Socrates as an inspiring image of restless striving for faith. It is extremely difficult to know how much you can do or learn if you give it your best effort, so that many people quit long before they accomplish all that they could. Kierkegaard thinks that it is our duty to strive for the ideal, and that almost all of us fail to strive as strenuously as we could and should. Moreover, he thinks that many people who think they are Christians do not strive strenuously to fulfill their duties, because they mistakenly believe that they rely properly on grace. But, Kierkegaard responds, they may be taking grace in vain; for it is very unlikely that a person can learn to rely on grace without first striving with all their might, failing, and learning their utter need for God. You do not really discover your need for God until you encounter your own weakness through heroic but unsuccessful effort. What is more, Kierkegaard teaches that the purpose of grace is not to render striving unnecessary, but to support it and to make it successful. God gives grace to help people strive, not to make them lazy and cozy. The figure of Socrates in Kierkegaard's authorship is a heroic image of the restless, daemonic, transgressive, and prophetic striving that Kierkegaard thinks is the duty and destiny of all human beings.

Socrates represents in Kierkegaard's writings the baptism of human reason and of other noble aspects of paganism. He also symbolizes the redemption of esthetics, which is centered on the beautiful and the interesting. One might have thought that the interesting and the heroic were rather at odds with one another. Nietzsche thought so. For cunning, crime, deception, and inconsistencies of character can be very interesting, while heroes tend to be simple and forthright fellows. But when the heroic and the interesting are combined in the most cunningly ironic but also most honest intellectual hero, namely, "that simple wise man of old" who "deceived people into the truth," the result is "the most interesting man who ever lived."

Johannes de Silentio writes that Socrates had to *acquire* his interesting *existence* with "trouble and pain" (FT 83). This is to say that Socrates became interesting through his heroic striving. There are several ways that Socrates unites the heroic and the interesting. By striving heroically he creates an interesting tension between his infinite goal and the finitude of his human self, his circumstances, and his progress towards his goal. He also makes heroic efforts partly to conceal that he helps other people to become the heroes of their own lives, and the tension between this concealment and his partial revelation of himself makes him all the more interesting. We can also understand his unification of the heroic and interesting by reflecting on his way of relating to limits. On the one hand, he honestly admits his failures, dwells in his limits in order to express reverence for God, and deviously conceals the assistance that he gives to other human beings in order to avoid playing God and tempting them to idolize him. On the other hand, he strives to transcend his limits, because, though he knows how little or how much he has accomplished, he does not know the limits of what he could accomplish; nor does he know how much his daemon or perhaps even "the god" might help him to achieve if he makes himself receptive to divine aid. This tension between his submission to his limits and his ambitious efforts to surpass them makes him the most interesting man who ever lived.[7]

---

7. For a fuller account of Socrates see McCombs, *Paradoxical Rationality of Søren Kierkegaard*, chapters 6 and 7.

CHAPTER SIX

Contemporaneity with Christ

KIERKEGAARD'S TASK AS AN author may be described as "introducing Christianity into Christendom." Reflecting on this task, one might reasonably expect Kierkegaard and his pseudonyms to talk often about Christ, since Christianity is after all about Christ. But this reasonable expectation proves to be false. Consider the case of Johannes de Silentio. Curiously, although he writes about Christian faith, he pens only one paragraph about Christ, and neglects to mention the crucial fact that Christ is the object of Christian faith. Silentio, it seems, is quite reticent to talk about Christ, or even to mention him. Johannes Climacus writes much more than Silentio does about Christ, and stresses that Christ is the object of faith. But he never mentions Jesus Christ by name in *Fragments*. Instead he speaks coyly of the *hypothesis* of the "god man," and he admits that *Fragments* is about Christianity only in the last pages of his book. Therefore, Climacus too is reticent to talk about Christ. And so is Kierkegaard himself, mostly. Given the importance of a believer's relation to Christ, one might have expected Kierkegaard to create a pseudonym who exemplifies this relation. But, surprisingly, there is no such pseudonym in Kierkegaard's writings.

Why then is Kierkegaard so reticent to speak about Christ? Basically, he thinks that to talk directly about him by name is often unhelpful, or even harmful. Almost all of Kierkegaard's readers, he thinks, have deeply ingrained prejudices about and misunderstandings of Christ. Almost all people have habitual emotional reactions to Christ that Kierkegaard thinks are inadequate, inappropriate, or sinful. If this is true, then a person who writes directly about Christ, even the most beautiful and true words about him, is unlikely get his message across or to achieve the results at which he aims. He would say one thing, and his readers would hear something else. He might express Christian passions of wonder, gratitude, and adoration, but many of his readers might feel something else entirely, boredom, perhaps, or annoyance, or sentimental nostalgia. If he were to explain directly that he was trying to correct common errors about Christ and Christianity, many people would not be receptive to this correction, and would persist in their misunderstanding. Given these difficulties, how is a wise person to write about Christ and Christianity? According to Kierkegaard, wisdom in this matter proceeds deviously and indirectly. When he writes about Christ, Kierkegaard often avoids traditional Christian terminology, which is apt to be misunderstood, and which is likely to trigger hackneyed emotional responses that are not worthy of Christ. Instead he ingeniously invents new ways of talking about old things in order to circumvent his readers' defenses and thus win a hearing. Since his readers see Christianity as something tired and worn out, he reinvents it and rejuvenates it for them, so that they can see it as if for the first time, and feel passions about it that are worthy of it. In short, he seeks to replace their insipid clichés about Christianity with a primitive impression of the wondrous story that God became incarnate as an individual human being.

Kierkegaard's reticence about Christ means that he refrains from creating a pseudonym who describes, first person, his own life of faith. The reason for his reticence is that he thinks everyone must achieve such a life for himself or herself. To speak as or for an exemplary believer would be presumptuous meddling. Everyone must work out his own salvation in fear and trembling, with no helper except God, who works in him both to will and to work. Kierkegaard helps people develop the capacities by which they can become properly aware of Christ. But then he leaves it up to them to use these capacities for themselves. Because he respects the freedom, personal responsibility, and heroic vocation of his readers, he does not interfere with their essentially solo task of becoming single individuals alone before God.

Several years after creating Johannes Climacus, Kierkegaard created a pseudonym named Anti-Climacus, who, in *Practice in Christianity*, frequently uses the words "Jesus Christ," who often talks about the nature of a personal relation to Christ, who addresses Christ personally as *you*, and who writes prayers to Christ. This pseudonym also imagines many characters who relate to Christ in various defective ways. But he does not describe his own personal relation to Christ, or the first-person relation of

Contemporaneity with Christ

any believer to the object of faith. By the way, the scholarly consensus on the meaning of Anti-Climacus's name is not that he is *opposed to* or *against* Johannes Climacus, but that he comes *before* Johannes in the sense of being *superior to* him.[1]

Anti-Climacus has several things going against him. He is severe, demanding, and offensive, like a Hebrew prophet who decries the people's sins, makes stringent demands on them in the name of God, and therefore tempts them to stone him. Owing to Anti-Climacus's likeness to such a prophet, it is easy to want to castigate him more than one wants to praise him. Many readers of Anti-Climacus might say that he is boring, or would be boring, if he were not so offensive and disturbing. He certainly does not seem to have captivated the imagination of scholars, who have written much less about him than about the books of Silentio and Climacus. It seems to me, however, that Anti-Climacus is the most boldly imaginative of all Kierkegaard's pseudonyms, and I would like to argue for this claim a little in this present chapter. As for his harshness, I will leave it to you to read him and determine for yourself whether it is excessive or appropriate.

Anti-Climacus is like Johannes Climacus in his concern for the *issue* of "becoming a Christian." But, whereas Johannes writes about this issue at a somewhat comfortable distance, Anti-Climacus presents it with great urgency. Anti-Climacus explains that to become a Christian one must become "contemporary with Christ." Part of what he means by this contemporaneity is to "*see* Christ as you are," "in your true form and in the surroundings of actuality as you walked here on earth" (PC 9). To see Christ as he is and in his true form is a very ambitious goal. But Anti-Climacus clearly thinks he can accomplish it. For he repeatedly claims that Christ *must* do some deed or other, or *cannot* perform this or that action, as though Anti-Climacus rigorously knows the nature or essence of Christ. Obviously, if he knows Christ's essence, then he sees Christ in his true form. Kierkegaard often claims that he writes "without authority," and presumably Anti-Climacus too would say this about himself. But, as we shall see, in his knowledge-claims about Christ Anti-Climacus comes pretty close to an assertion of authority. If he knows so well who Christ is and what Christianity requires, then he has a sort of authority, even if he has not been annointed by God for a special mission.

---

1. See Howard and Edna Hong's "Historical Introduction" to *The Sickness Unto Death*, xxii.

What then is the true form of Christ in the surroundings of actuality as he walked here on earth? In short, love. Anti-Climacus stresses that Christ loved human beings, and that out of love he wanted to help them and offered to help them. Anti-Climacus movingly describes Christ's love and his sufferings when people were offended by his love and rejected his attempts to help them. One reason that people were offended by his loving offers of help is that he was as "poor as the poorest" human being, who owned nothing but his clothes, and who seemed to be more in need of assistance himself than almost all people (13). It is offensive when a person who appears inferior to you offers to do some great good for you. But the offensiveness does not end here. Suppose that a person is able to glimpse the spiritual superiority of Christ, and manages to accept Christ's offer of help. Then it turns out that the only or primary assistance that Christ gives is the forgiveness of sins, or some such thing (61). It is offensive to be called a sinner, and it is offensive to be offered assistance and then be informed that the only assistance in the offering is the forgiveness of sins. This bait and switch might feel like a perfidious betrayal. Suppose then that a person manages not to be offended by any of this, and gratefully accepts the forgiveness of sins. Then he is informed that he must strive to imitate Christ, with the result that, like Christ, he will be hated, mocked, reviled, spat upon, ostracized, persecuted, or perhaps even crucified. But to strive to be divinely good, and then to be punished as a devilish evildoer, is extremely offensive. Far be it from God, one thinks, to allow such gross injustice to befall a sincere imitator of Christ.

The chief cause of offense, according to Anti-Climacus, is the difficulty of coming to terms with the paradox that Christ is infinitely *lofty* and extremely *lowly*. On the night of his arrest, Christ correctly predicted to his disciples that they would all soon be offended at him. The reason for their offense was that they had glimpsed his loftiness, and they could not understand how the Messiah and the Son of God could be so meek and weak as to allow himself to be captured by the authorities and abused by them. The disciples thought the lofty one should triumph, not be despised and disgraced. Most of Christ's contemporaries, according to Anti-Climacus, were offended at Christ in a way which was exactly opposite to the way the disciples were. That is, they saw the lowly Christ, who was the son of a carpenter, lacking in political authority, poor, and, most importantly, seemingly a mere man. Then this mere man spoke and acted as if he was God, or even claimed to be God, and people were offended at this seemingly outrageous claim. To be sure, they were impressed by him as a teacher and as a lover of humanity. If they had thought he was simply a madman, they would not have been offended that he claimed to be God. But since he was wise and loving, and then claimed to be God, he put them in a bind, and in this predicament they suffered and were in many cases offended.

Anti-Climacus illuminatingly compares offense to envy. Envy, he says, occurs when a person *admires* a superior person, but cannot *happily surrender* to this feeling of inferiority, and therefore instead chooses to be resentfully pained by other's superiority and excellence (SUD 86). It is the same, he says, with offense. Suppose that someone has intimations of the divinity of Christ, so that it would become possible for him to adore and worship him. But, if this person cannot happily surrender to their feelings of veneration, they will then take offense. No doubt you perceive that Anti-Climacus sees this refusal to adore Christ as the result of pride. The proud person does not want to be the inferior one, or the obedient one, but to be great and independent of God. Sensing the greatness of Christ gives intensity to one's response to him. The person who acutely perceives Christ's possible divinity and surrenders in obedient worship experiences great joy. But the person who acutely perceives Christ's possible divinity, and refuses to worship, is intensely offended. Anti-Climacus names the most extreme offense *defiance* and *the demonic*. The demonic person is so strong in his defiance that he would rather voluntarily suffer the worst agony than to ask for and receive loving assistance from God. The descriptions of a demoniac given by Anti-Climacus in *The Sickness Unto Death* make for disturbing reading (70–74).

Anti-Climacus asserts that faith and offense are the only adequate responses to Christ. One might have thought that calm and reasoned disbelief, or impartial doubt, or cautious suspension of judgment, was an adequate response. Not so, insists Anti-Climacus, who argues that Christ himself was deeply concerned about the possibility of offense, since he repeatedly warned against the danger of offense in the following words: "Blessed is he who is not offended in me" (SUD 128). Anti-Climacus reasons something like this about Christ's words: "Given that Christ may be depended on to speak precisely and with care, it is crucial that he did say the blessed were people who did not *doubt* him, but people who were not *offended* at him. His word-choice implies that rejecting him responsibly cannot be the result of honest doubt, but is instead the result of offense, so that the authentic options on the question of Christ are not belief or doubt, but faith or offense."

If the choice about Christ, rightly made, is a choice between faith and offense, it follows that faith requires resisting the temptation to be offended. In order to *choose between* faith and offense, a person must perceive the attractiveness of both options. With this requirement in mind, Anti-Climacus draws the conclusion that the person who proclaims Christianity is not permitted to hide or gloss over the possibility of offense, and must even stress it. In their presentations of Christianity, both Anti-Climacus and Kierkegaard emphasize aspects of Christianity that are potentially offensive, like Christ's combination of loftiness and lowliness, and a human being's need to have his sins forgiven.

Anti-Climacus gives a striking name to the situation in which a person becomes so profoundly aware of Christ that it becomes necessary to choose between faith and offense, namely, "contemporaneity with Christ." Kierkegaard thought that during his time people failed to become contemporary with Christ because they had heard so much foolish chatter about him, and had inherited false ideas about him. He also thought that, in order to overcome this foolishness and falsity, and draw near to the reality of Christ, there was need to imagine what it would be like to encounter Christ in person. When someone adequately imagines this encounter, Kierkegaard and Anti-Climacus say that he has become "contemporary with Christ."

Anti-Climacus does not imaginatively describe what it is like to be a believer who is contemporary with Christ. Nor does he imaginatively describe what it is like to be intensely offended at Christ in the situation of contemporaneity. But he does imaginatively describe, at length, ten instances of mild offense; and this description lays a foundation for his readers to build on (PC 42–52). His description of mild offense is noteworthy in several respects. First, he has each of the ten offended people speak for themselves. By doing this, he reveals offense vividly and from the inside. Someone who cannot see himself in an abstract description of offense may be able to see himself in a poetic first-person expression of it. Second, there is considerable variety in the ten offended people who speak for themselves. Perhaps a reader will not see himself in one or in many of them. But he is likely to resemble at least one of them. The abundant variety in the ten offended fellows increases the likelihood that readers can discover their own offense in at least one of the ten. The multiplicity of descriptions might also reveal to readers that they themselves are offended in a variety of ways. Third, Anti-Climacus transposes Christ to nineteenth century Copenhagen, where the ten people who take offense at him encounter him. Since many readers lack the imagination to become contemporary with Christ as he was in ancient Palestine, Anti-Climacus makes Christ contemporary with them in their own present age. Given that they cannot travel to him, Anti-Climacus brings him to them. And he goes even further than this. Since some readers will not adequately imagine the offense that they would take at a contemporary Christ, Anti-Climacus describes for them in many ways how they might take offense. A nineteenth-century reader who could not discover his resemblance to even one of these ten examples of offense would have to be stubbornly blind indeed.

Anti-Climacus does not give titles to five of these characters, whom he describes as *sagacious* and *sensible*. Like most people, they are ruled by "finite common sense." Owing to their superficial attitudes about the most momentous things, their comments are rather comical, as you will see. One of them is so frivolous that he wonders how Christ is preparing for his old age, and notes that the Messiah does not even know how to play cards! Another is sufficiently perceptive to discern that Christ has a profound wisdom, which he thinks Christ does not use rightly. He wonders whether he could *trick* Christ "out of his wisdom," and use it for his own worldly purposes. Another thinks that it is foolish humility for Christ to associate with the poor and downtrodden, who cannot help him to acquire prestige and political power. It would be better, thinks this person, for Christ to associate with the rich and influential people among his generation. These five untitled characters are unanimous in refusing to take Christ's claim to be God seriously. This refusal has the effect of making their offense comically mild or mediocre. Presumably Anti-Climacus thinks that their mild offense mirrors that of most of his contemporaries, who do not rise to demonic intensity, or sink to demonic depths, but coast comfortably on the surface of things. The other five characters include a clergyman, a philosopher, a statesman, a solid citizen, and a scoffer. The sagacious statesmen perceives that Christ is a threat to the established order, and how dangerous it would be to make public statements about Christ, and he therefore resolves to keep quiet as he waits for *the result*. The philosopher is the only character who is sufficiently spirited to be very annoyed that Christ claims to be God. Most of the ten characters sensibly predict that Christ will not come to a good end. Presumably this prediction has much to do with their cowardly refusal to come near to Christ, and thereby risk being dragged down with him in his *downfall*.

Poetry and Heroism

There is a young man in Kierkegaard's *Repetition* who imaginatively tells himself the story of Job from diverse points of view and in "the most diverse ways" (R 204). Anti-Climacus similarly tells Christ's story in many ways, and interprets Christ's words "from various sides," in order to help his readers to become aware of who Christ is (PC 259). One particularly illuminating way that he retells the story of Christ is that he asks his readers to imagine a child who does not know about the Messiah. He does this to sweep away the chatter of the ages and thus arrive at an authentically primitive impression of the founder of Christianity. For a child thinks about things simply, naively, and naturally. Then Anti-Climacus asks the reader to imagine telling Christ's story to the child. This also is a sound strategy, since we work harder to understand and appreciate a story when we tell it. Then Anti-Climacus shows how he himself would tell the child about Christ's life, and imagines the response of the child, who would be much more concerned about Christ's sufferings than he was inspired by Christ's glory, and would wonder sorrowfully that God in heaven did nothing to prevent the crucifixion. Then Anti-Climacus goes on to imagine how the child would continue to ponder Christ as he grew older. In short, Climacus uses the child to model someone who looks as Christ freshly and is therefore more struck by the lowliness and sufferings of Christ than by his glorious loftiness (174–79).

The difference between the young man's modest meditations on Job in *Repetition* and the daring meditations of Anti-Climacus's about Christ in *Practice in Christianity* is astonishing. Because the young man believes that he is vastly inferior to Job, he refrains from *making Job's words his own* in the presence of another person, or even in writing, though he does this when he is *alone* (R 204). As we shall see, Anti-Climacus is so much bolder than the young man that he (almost) makes the words of Christ his own, in print. At the least he speaks with great confidence when he explains the meaning of Christ's words, as if he were their author. How can it be that Anti-Climacus presumes to appropriate words of Christ in a book, when the young man does not even dare to appropriate words of Job in a private letter to a friend?

Anti-Climacus writes that Christ "does not want to be judged humanly by the results of his life, because he is and wants to be the sign of offense and the object of faith" (PC 23). It seems that Anti-Climacus thinks he is privy the Christ's thoughts. We might even say that he claims to state the essence or "true form" of Christ and of his words and purposes. Consider also these words of Anti-Climacus: "Ah, abysmal suffering, unfathomable to human understanding—to have to be the sign of offense in order to be the object of faith!" (105). Christ does not explicitly speak of this suffering and its cause. It is Anti-Climacus who infers, or clairvoyantly perceives, this suffering, its depth, and its cause. Admittedly, Anti-Climacus implies that he does not quite fathom the suffering of Christ. But he seems to think that he sees pretty deeply, and that he knows where to dig—namely, in the vein of suffering caused to divine love by the necessity of being a sign of offense in order to be the object of faith. Anti-Climacus writes that "in order to understand someone's statement" one needs to understand the *mood* in which the words are said (163). In compliance with this requirement for understanding, he goes about telling us in what mood Christ said his words about offense. Christ does not himself name his mood, but Anti-Climacus prophetically perceives that it is *suffering love*. What great imaginative power Anti-Climacus must think he has! What great imaginative power he expects his readers to employ in order to understand his interpretation of Christ! Examples could be multiplied of Anti-Climacus's bold confidence in the capacity of imagination to place a modern person, not only in the situation of contemporaneity with Christ, but in the mind of Christ. But we will move on to a consideration of his most outrageously daring use of imagination.

Anti-Climacus reminds us that Christ offended people by telling them that they must eat his flesh and drink his blood in order to have life in themselves. When many of his followers are offended by this hard saying and leave him, Christ "says to the twelve" disciples, "'do you also wish to go away?'" Anti-Climacus detects great suffering in these words, suffering grounded in the sad necessity that in order to help people, Christ must risk pushing them away. Then Anti-Climacus claims that when Christ says those words, "it is almost as if he were to say: Shall I, then, I who came to save all, I whose love no human being, none at all, comprehends, shall I be brought to this, that I would become the salvation of no one at all" (PC 100). In this passage we see Anti-Climacus not only making Christ's words his own, but inventing words for Christ! Relying on statistics in ethical or religious meditation is often a symptom of superficial thinking, but I cannot help noticing that in the three lines that Anti-Climacus invents for Christ, he uses the word "I" five times. That is a lot of I-saying for three lines when you are inventing a speech for Christ! Admittedly, Anti-Climacus is cautious enough to preface his impersonation of divinity by saying it is "almost as if" Christ were to say the lines that Anti-Climacus composes for him. That "almost as if" is perhaps enough to prevent the impersonation from being blatantly blasphemous. If "no one can look on God and live," what happens to someone who almost as if invents words and attributes them to Christ. If we set aside Anti-Climacus's audacious flirtation with blasphemy in the service of piety, I think we can agree that the speech he almost attributes to Christ is powerful and moving, and that it might perhaps express divine thoughts and sentiments. But the main point here is not how well Anti-Climacus impersonates Christ, but that he dares to impersonate him at all. How great a contrast there is between Silentio, who could only manage to mention Christ once when talking about Christian faith, and Anti-Climacus, who writes lines for Christ to say, in a religious drama about divine love, human offense, and divine suffering! Kierkegaard and his pseudonyms often use the phrase, *humanly speaking*. In his speech-writing for Christ Anti-Climacus could have said, *divinely speaking*, and meant it.

Anti-Climacus calls imagination the "capacity *instar omnium*," the capacity for all capacities, and he sees it as essential for becoming contemporary with Christ (SUD 31). But he does not regard it as sufficient for contemporaneity. For speaks of the "distance of imagination" and contrasts this distance with the truth of *actuality* "in the situation of contemporaneity" (100). If you are contemporaneous with Christ in imagination, you have indeed drawn near to him. But not near enough, unless you go further than mere religious poetry. What else then is needed? First of all, a person must *will* to draw near, and not just imaginatively flirt with proximity. According to Kierkegaard, when you "read God's Word," "you must incessantly say to yourself" that "it is I to whom it is speaking" and "it is I about whom it is speaking" (FSE 40). You should allow God's Word to address *you* as a single individual. Anti-Climacus tries to win our compliance with this rule by often addressing his readers as *you*. Another means to nearness to Christ is become aware that if one finds oneself loving Christ, the next step is to imitate him, by living and suffering like him. Becoming aware of, and acknowledging, this invitation or summons to imitate Christ brings one's will closer to Christ. A person must also scrupulously and honestly *examine* and "pay attention" to their reaction to the story of Christ, and not rely on clichés or the chatter of the ages, in order to learn his or her own response (39, 97). Constantine Constantius ridicules people who attend the theater, and then read reviews of the play in the next morning's newspaper to determine whether or not they enjoyed themselves the previous evening

(R 160). So much do people rely on others in deciding how to think and feel! Anti-Climacus urges you not to depend on other people to know how you think and feel about Christ, but to pay attention to yourself in the situation of contemporaneity in order to discover your authentic, personal response to Christ. Finally, I think that Kierkegaard himself believes in a sort of mysterious act of will by which a person draws near to God in their very being. Obviously it is hard to say anything clear and solid about this divine encounter, but I am fairly sure Kierkegaard hints at it.

After trying many times and in many ways to evoke love in his readers for Christ, by retelling the story of Christ's love for humanity, Anti-Climacus imagines that he has not succeeded, and that his reader does not feel grateful love for Christ. Then the usually stern and severe Anti-Climacus becomes surprisingly lenient when he gently encourages the reader not to give up, not to *despair*, but to keep trying to see Christ in such a way that the vision evokes love (179).

You have probably noticed that we have not discussed any heroines, poetesses, or female pseudonyms in Kierkegaard's authorship. He in fact creates no female pseudonyms, perhaps out of modesty. He and his pseudonyms do, however, sometimes praise heroines. Silentio, for example, praises Mary, the mother of Jesus, very highly, and he insists that Sarah, not Tobias, is the truly heroic character in the book of *Tobit* (FT 65; 102–4). There are other examples, but it must be admitted that there are few heroines in Kierkegaard's authorship. Silentio explicitly says that women as much as men can be knights of faith (45). But there are also some possibly disparaging or disrespectful remarks about women in Kierkegaard's corpus. It would be difficult to determine exactly what his theory of the sexes is, or even to decide whether he is consistent in what he says about women and men.

The most notable exception to Kierkegaard's neglect of heroines is that he wrote three "Christian Discourses" about "the woman who was a sinner" from the Gospel of Luke, chapter 7. She is perhaps the greatest model provided by Kierkegaard of a faithful relation to Christ. I will end this chapter by saying a little about Kierkegaard's beautiful and moving praise of this heroine.

Kierkegaard calls her a *guide* and a *prototype*, and this is to say that she is heroic (WA 143, 144). According to him, she exemplifies several heroic virtues and deeds, for example, not despairing when she is in a situation that would tempt anyone to despair. She is also a model of drawing near to

Christ, both metaphorically and literally. Literally she approaches Christ when he is at a gathering of Pharisees, whose contempt for and animosity toward her are so great that it is as if Christ were locked up in "an impregnable fortress" (154). But she manages to infiltrate it. Most importantly, she is an exemplar of love for Christ. Kierkegaard says that he would like to love God and his Savior just as she does (142). She also exemplifies "proper sorrow over one's sin," without which a person cannot properly pray for and receive forgiveness (142). Finally, she is a model of a crucial spiritual realization that Kierkegaard talks about often in his authorship, namely, that without God "I am capable of literally nothing at all" (143). That is why "to need God," or to be aware that one needs God and to rely on God, "is a human being's highest perfection" (EUD 297). An important aspect of her need for God is that "one thing is unconditionally important to her, to find forgiveness" in Christ (WA 154). Her urgent need for forgiveness is what gives her the courage to draw near to Christ in the hostile presence of the Pharisees. Many people, according to Kierkegaard, despair over their sins, or over the possibility of the forgiveness of their sins, but she has the courage and the humility to silently beseech Christ for forgiveness, even though conventional moralizing might counsel her to despair owing to the gravity of her sins. It is remarkable that in the story as Luke tells it the woman does not say anything at all, but weeps, and washes Christ's feet, with her tears, her hair, and costly myrrh. Kierkegaard regards her *silence* as a virtue, not because she is a woman and women should be silent, but because for everyone, woman or man, silence before God is greater than any speech—for it expresses humble readiness to hear every word that comes from the mouth of God (149, 10–14).

It turns out, then, that Kierkegaard does in fact present one exemplary model of how to relate to Christ: the woman who was a sinner. But he talks about her in the third person, and she does not speak for herself, or even talk at all. Her silence is humble receptivity in the presence of her savior. Kierkegaard's refusal to speak for the exemplary believer is similarly a modest reticence, and a humble avoidance of pretending to be more for his fellow human beings than he thinks it is fitting or possible for him to be.

CHAPTER SEVEN

Kierkegaard as Truth Witness and as Single Individual

As "A POET WHO influences by means of the ideals," Kierkegaard is a strict taskmaster who repeatedly proclaims variations of Christ's frightfully demanding commandment to "be perfect, as your Father in heaven is perfect."[1] For example, in *Practice in Christianity* he writes that "the requirement for being a Christian is forced up by the pseudonymous author to a supreme ideality" (PC 7). Kierkegaard worries a lot about the following questions: if he himself is far from attaining the ideals, does his proclaiming them with severity make him a hypocrite, and does his defectiveness give others an excuse to ignore or dismiss the supremely ideal requirements? If he is not himself a hero, but demands heroism of his readers, is he like the Pharisees whom Christ castigates for *loading* people with *burdens* that are "hard to bear," when they themselves do not so much as *touch* the burdens "with one of their fingers"?[2]

Kierkegaard repeatedly says that he is "only a poet," by which he means that he does not put himself forward as a model of what he praises (TM 226). This description of himself as a mere poet implies that he does not regard himself as heroic. But, when he confesses that he is only a poet, he also sometimes adds that he *defines* himself "as one who is striving" (JP 6 6528). By calling himself a striver, he suggests that he is after all heroic. For the most important quality of a hero according to Kierkegaard is striving

1. Matt 5:48.
2. Luke 11:46.

or struggling. So maybe he does in fact regard himself as heroic. Consider these grandiose words that he writes about himself: "my poet, who, when he comes, will usher me to the place among those who have suffered for an idea" (PV 95). These words cast all modesty aside, since a person who deserves a poet to praise him because of his sufferings for an idea is clearly a hero. After claiming that he has a place in the ranks of those who have suffered for an idea, he goes on to imagine what his poet will say about him, for almost three whole pages! In them Kierkegaard performs the function of his own poet by praising himself. We see, then, that Kierkegaard is sometimes modest, and sometimes speaks grandly about himself. Should we explain his conflicting self-descriptions by conjecturing that he is fickle or confused? Or is there a way in which his conflicting descriptions of himself can be harmonized with one another? I propose that Kierkegaard is in fact consistent, because, although he boldly implies he is a version of the kind of hero which he calls a "truth witness," he modestly denies being what he regards as the most important kind of hero, a "hero of faith."

My purpose in this chapter is not to praise Kierkegaard as a hero, or to denounce him as a mere pretender to heroism, or in general to assess his life and character. For I do not think I am worthy to set myself up as his judge. I will, however, relay to you some of the most common criticisms of his character and actions, and mention how one might begin to defend him against these accusations. Or, better, I will attempt to state some of the crucial questions to be explored by a confidently capable person who wishes to judge whether Kierkegaard is a hero, or a villain, or a little of both. More importantly, I will explain what kind of hero Kierkegaard claims to be, so that you may decide for yourselves whether this sort of heroism is admirable and worthy of imitation.

Kierkegaard calls a hero who suffers for an idea a "truth witness," or a witness to the truth (TM 5). The traditional term for this kind of hero is *martyr*, which means *witness* in ancient Greek. One of the most important virtues of truth witnessing is honesty. In his last writings, when Kierkegaard might perhaps best claim to be a truth witness, he says that what he wants more than anything else of his readers is *honesty*, and calls himself "a human honesty," which is a strange and striking phrase (TM 46).

What then is the idea to which Kierkegaard witnesses and for which he claims to suffer? He is quite clear that he does not claim to be a witness to the truth of Christianity, or to his faith in this truth. He thinks that being this kind of witness requires being an exemplary Christian, and he modestly refrains from claiming this about himself. What he most often witnesses to is the ideal of "the single individual." In this chapter we will consider three aspects of this ideal, and connect each of them to a famous episode in Kierkegaard's life.

First, Kierkegaard witnesses to the idea that every human being has a vocation to express allegiance to God as the greatest good and the highest authority, by being willing to suspend his or her allegiance to any lesser good in obedience to God. In other words, rightly relating to God makes every human being an *exception* to the laws of nations and to *universal* norms. Fulfilling your absolute duty to obey God can therefore bring you into painful conflict with other human beings whom you ought to love and respect. Second, as a single individual Kierkegaard witnesses that the "crowd is untruth" (PV 106). For in a crowd people conspire to avoid the rigors and responsibilities involved in becoming single individuals alone before God. The tumult of the crowd enables people to ignore the quiet voice of conscience, so that in a crowd people typically behave in ways they would find contemptible if they were honest with themselves in solitary reflection. The crowd, therefore, is untruth because it is the enemy of the ideal of single individuality. Owing to the opposing natures of the single individual and the crowd, they are fated to clash with one another, so that the single individual in opposition to the crowd cannot avoid being despised, mocked, shunned, or even persecuted. Third, Kierkegaard witnesses as a single individual that *Christendom* is an "enormous illusion" (23). By Christendom he means a sort of crowd writ large, or conventional nineteenth-century European society in its attempt to pass off its comfortable and watered down religiosity as authentic Christianity. Like every crowd, Christendom is a collective self-deception whose purpose is to conceal the difficult, strenuous, and heroic human vocation to become a single individual who exists alone before God.

We will now consider the three aspects of single individuality at greater length, beginning with the single individual as an *exception*. One of the most famous stories in the life of Kierkegaard is his romance with Regine Olson. After becoming engaged to her, he came to believe that their union would be disastrous. He judged that by marrying her he would unfairly burden her with his profound melancholy, his ill health, and a dreadful family secret that perhaps amounted almost to a curse. Therefore, he broke off the engagement in the hope that this would be acting for the best. Once he decided to back out of his promise, he fully exerted his considerable ingenuity in attempts to ease Regine's suffering, partly by pretending to be a scoundrel who had never loved her. It is natural for us to be curious about this juicy and scandalous story, and to wonder whether Kierkegaard behaved nobly in it, or, as might seem probable, like a cad. It seems to me difficult to decide. In order to judge well we would need to know the answers to several hard questions. Could and should Kierkegaard have known before proposing to Regine that marrying her would make her wretched? Was he correct that he would have made her miserable? Even if he was correct, should he nevertheless have married her if that is what she wanted when informed adequately of his fears? Was the complicated and devious way in which he attempted to wean Regine from him reasonable and honorable, or base and insane? In short, did he do the best he could have when he decided to marry Regine, and then not to marry her, and did he do his best to help her cope with his decision to cancel the engagement?

In any case, our business is with something other than judging a fellow human being: namely, *what* Kierkegaard learned from this dramatic and painful story in his life, and *how* he used what he learned. Kierkegaard's basic discovery from his romantic relation to Regine was that not all people can fulfill certain universal ethical norms, for example the biblical injunction to leave one's parents and to cleave to one's spouse. As a result, exceptional people are bound to clash painfully with others, and may then go on either to live in lonely resentment of the comfort other people derive from being members of society, or to find consolation in relating to God directly, that is, not through universal norms.

The genius of Kierkegaard shows itself in how he takes his own experience of being an exception, transmutes it into an ideal and a duty for everyone, and gives it a profound religious significance. Through the transmutation that Kierkegaard discovered, the exception becomes a person who perceives something higher than the universal, and who therefore clashes with the universal in order to serve that higher thing. A famous example of such a hero in Kierkegaard's writings is Abraham, who performs a "teleological suspension of the ethical" when he resolves to obey God's command to sacrifice his son Isaac, a command that contradicts the ethical prohibition against murder. Admittedly, Kierkegaard's own breach of the universal was not performed gloriously in service of something higher. But from his own less remarkable and unheroic clash with the universal, he discerned the possibility of a single individual called by God to express in his or her actions that the universal is not the greatest good, but that the relation to

God is the highest. The universal, both as ethical law and as the state, is to be sure a good thing, but not the greatest good. Although the universal is not the highest, it tends to become an idol. In order to oppose this idolatry, Kierkegaard became an iconoclast who asserted that the single individual alone before God is higher than the universal. For the individual, thinks Kierkegaard, has an eternal soul, while the state is doomed sooner or later to perish forever. Therefore, ethical laws are not ends in themselves, but are meant to serve loving communion with God and other human beings.

Although Kierkegaard did not renege on his marriage proposal to Regine in order to express the relativity of the universal and the absoluteness of the individual's relation to God, he voluntarily surrendered to the suffering that this reneging caused him; and by thinking profoundly about his experience in this matter he came to the conclusion that the greatest good for a human being is to be a single individual alone before God. Having learned this, he became an exception of sorts who was frequently in conflict with the universal in order to assert that, great and good though it was, it was not the highest. In short, through being an initially involuntary and unadmirable exception, Kierkegaard became a voluntary and at least somewhat admirable one, and therefore perhaps a hero. Heroism is not perfection, but struggling strenuously against imperfection. Kierkegaard seems to have struggled mightily against his imperfections, with the result that he wrought something useful and inspiring for many other people. Regine to be sure suffered from Kierkegaard's flaws, but many readers have benefited from what he learned from his errors. As a lover of Shakespeare, Kierkegaard might be delighted if the following words of a hopeful lover proved to be a prophecy about him: "They say, best men are molded out of faults; and, for the most, become much more the better for being a little bad."

The single individual is virtually the opposite of the crowd, and can be a single individual only by resisting the impulse to join ranks with the crowd. Kierkegaard expresses the relation between the single individual and the crowd in the following words: "this is my faith, that however much confusion and evil and contemptibleness there can be in human beings as soon as they become the irresponsible and unrepentant 'public', 'crowd', etc.—there is just as much truth and goodness and lovableness in them when one can get them as single individuals" (PV 10–11).

People join a crowd to avoid the task of becoming single individuals. They evade responsibility by *comparing* themselves with others. They think that if they are like the others, or that if they are average, or maybe a little better—and who isn't—that is good enough. People in a crowd elude responsibility by sharing it and thereby infinitely diluting it. Responsibility must remain intact or it is nothing, as the baby that Solomon cunningly threatened to sever in twain had to remain whole in order to be what it was. People in a crowd behave worse than they would on their own because of bad examples, safety in numbers, a flattering feeling of power, their resentment of superiors, the opportunity to tear down excellence, and a desire to escape boredom through cheap excitement. They behave badly but don't feel guilty about it because they are only doing what everyone else is doing. They do not listen to their consciences before they act, so as to choose rightly; and if they act wrongly, they do not listen to their consciences in order to repent. Therefore, Kierkegaard says, "the crowd is untruth" (PV 106). In a crowd people have lost the dignity of being human persons, or of being what Kierkegaard calls *selves*. They have lost the truth of human nature, and they almost congratulate one another for their common loss.

A single individual is true, good, and lovable because she attentively listens in solitude *to* the claims of duty and *for* the voice of God sounding in her conscience. She takes responsibility for her actions and for the sort of person that she has become and is becoming. Since she does not attempt to share her responsibility with others, she feels the full weight of it, as well as the attention of God upon her every thought and deed; and this conscientiousness is the basis of her striving with all her might to fulfill the demands of duty.

A single individual must always fight against the urge to participate in the crimes of the crowd, and sometimes must go further and actively resist the crowd. That is, sometimes the single individual discovers a duty to stand up to the anonymous public, in order to test or express his resolve to be a single individual, or in order to reveal that whereas the crowd is untruth, there is truth in the single individual.

A famous run-in that Kierkegaard had with a newspaper called the *Corsair* illustrates his ideas about the relation of the single individual to the crowd. Kierkegaard saw the *Corsair* as a symbol of the crowd, because it was without conscience in slandering, caricaturing, and persecuting its sometimes innocent, sometimes guilty, victims, and because it pandered to the mob's worst appetites. The mob or public for its part indecently relished the unethical articles of the *Corsair*, but did not feel responsible for purchasing it, reading it, gossiping about its contents, mocking its victims, participating in its activity, and in general encouraging its wicked behavior.

Appalled at the behavior of the *Corsair*, Kierkegaard stepped forward into the lists and challenged the newspaper to attack him—which it did, with very painful results for him. The paper mocked his ideas, his books, his broken engagement, his presumed vanity about his talent, his misshapen back, and the unfashionable appearance of his trousers as they hung on his legs of uneven length. A crucial issue for anyone attempting to judge Kierkegaard's invitation for the *Corsair* to persecute him is his motive. Was he actuated by a superficial desire for attention? Did he vainly desire the glory of winning a war of wit with the *Corsair* ? Did masochism play a role in his inviting the newspaper to abuse him? Or did he see an evil in the world and bravely step forward to reveal its cruelty, mendacity, and inhuman irresponsibility? In short, was exposing the press's and the public's lack of conscience worth the cost of tempting them to sin against him? In any case, Kierkegaard's sufferings at the hands of the *Corsair* and the public taught him a great deal, and inspired the rich yield that consists of the whole second half of his authorship. I think we must acknowledge that the "*Corsair* Affair" made the conscienceless irresponsibility of the press and the public crystal clear to any honest observer.[3]

We will now consider the idea of the single individual as it relates to Kierkegaard's task of introducing Christianity into a nineteenth-century Denmark that labored under the illusion that it was authentically Christian. Kierkegaard thinks that single individuality is essential both to Christianity and to spreading its good news in the press-mad modern world: "*The single individual*—this category has been used only once, its first time, in a decisively dialectical way, by Socrates, in order to disintegrate paganism. In Christendom it will be used a second time in the very opposite way, to make people (the Christians) Christians" (PV 123). Kierkegaard encourages single individuality by addressing the conscience of his readers. He attempts to show people that conventional nineteenth-century society is not authentic Christianity. He seeks to teach people what Christianity really is, and how to become Christians. Real Christianity, he argues, is the most difficult task in the world. It demands perfection. It demands dying before you die. It demands such great commitment to the cause of Christianity that you should rejoice if you are persecuted for that cause. The motive for the enormous illusion of Christendom is a sort of conspiracy to water

---

3. See Howard and Edna Hong's "Historical Introduction" to the *Corsair Affair* for an account and interpretation of the relevant events in this episode in the life of Kierkegaard, vii–xxxviii.

down Christianity in order to make it easy and comfortable. Kierkegaard as a single individual attacks this enormous illusion to promote salutary enlightenment about it.

Kierkegaard's most famous witness to the monstrous illusion of Christendom consists of a series of newspaper articles and pamphlets that he published in the last year of his life. These writings have been aptly called the *Attack Upon Christendom*, and they are immensely controversial. Their tone is, at best, severe and harsh, or, at worst, judgmental and uncharitable. Many lovers of Kierkegaard deem that he went too far in his attack, and perhaps he did.[4] But it is well to remember that the Hebrew prophets were similarly harsh and severe, as was Jesus himself. It seems to me that if Kierkegaard knew that he was right about Christianity and Christendom, then he may have been justified in attacking Christendom so vehemently. Perhaps people needed that vehemence in order to be awakened from their delusions. Kierkegaard claims that he "know[s] with uncommon clarity and definiteness what Christianity is," and if he does know this, then perhaps he is right to act like an indignant and illusion-denouncing prophet (138). In order to judge that Kierkegaard was mistaken when he severely attacked Christendom, a person might have to know either that Kierkegaard is wrong about what Christianity is (when he claims to know what it is with exceptional clarity), or to know that widespread delusion about the nature of Christianity does not merit extreme polemics. One would also need to be well-informed about the situation in Denmark when Kierkegaard made his attack, and this would require more than familiarity with recent books on Kierkegaard that already digest and interpret the myriad facts of the case.

I think that Kierkegaard himself would say that the key question here concerns love. That is, did he attack Christendom out of love, or did he attack it out of demonic pride and hatred of people? Or is there a third possibility? Could something between demonic pride and hatred, on the one hand, and tough love on the other, explain Kierkegaard's impersonation of a Hebrew prophet? Could his attack be the result of a relatively innocent mistake, the result, that is, of a slightly blameworthy error? I myself think that would be very strange interpretation of the *Attack Upon Christendom*.

There are some errors concerning Kierkegaard's concept of the single individual that are easy to fall into. One might think that through this concept he affirms a vain and selfish display of one's idiosyncrasies, or that

---

4. For a charitable critic of Kierkegaard's behavior in his attack upon Christendom see Evans, *Kierkegaard and Spirituality*, 187–93.

he denies the worth of cooperation, community, politics, and society. But in fact he thinks that being a single individual means denying one's pride and vanity, and uniting in love with one's neighbor. His book *Works of Love* teaches how a single individual must lovingly unite with his or her fellow human beings, usually one-on-one. Kierkegaard claims that the "established order" tends to deify itself in order to escape the sovereignty of God, and therefore needs to be chastened. But he is not wholly negative about politics, as the following quotation shows: "the religious is eternity's transfigured rendition of the most beautiful dream of politics," or "of what a politician, provided he actually loves being a human being and loves humankind, has thought in his most blissful moment" (PV 103). If politics beautifully dreams of a community of people who love one another and worship God together, then it might be redeemable and should not be dismissed *tout court* as an abomination.

In summary, the single individual alone before God must be willing to play several roles in relation to groups of people and the rules by which they live. Sometimes she should affirm the universal as good, worthy of allegiance, and a propaedeutic for greater things. Sometimes she should be an exception who violates the laws of the universal so as to assert that there is something greater and higher than it. Sometimes, when the state or society suffers under the illusion that it is Christian, the single individual should attack it in order to expose its illusion, and this attack might require using harsh and severe methods to get people's attention. In fact the single individual might do any number of highly surprising things, getting her guidance as she does not only from ordinary morality, or conventional beliefs, but also sometimes from a profound conscientious sense of her individual mission in the world, or even perhaps from the voice of God spoken to her in secret.

I imagine it is the dream of many a scholar to fulfill the prophecy, and serve as the poet who ushers Kierkegaard to his place among those who have suffered for an idea. This poet would need to be almost the equal of Kierkegaard. He or she would have to understand Kierkegaard profoundly, become contemporary with him in imagination, generously sympathize with him, and have the gift of poetic composition. Perhaps this poet will indeed some day come. For now his ambitious admirers can only dream.

But not all readers of Kierkegaard aspire to be his poet. Some want to criticize or even denounce him. His uncompromising idealism, his polemical mission against his age, and the severity that he believed these things required, were sure to arouse ire and indignation among people who disagree with him about fundamentals, and who would be happy to have a plausible pretext to castigate him. Even some of his admirers reluctantly find fault with his attack upon Christendom.

Regardless of how we judge him, or whether we dare to judge him, Kierkegaard's harsh and controversial criticisms of his age illustrate his idea of the single individual, which is a disturbingly admirable species of hero. Whether or not he himself should have a place in the ranks of heroes who suffered for an ideal, he poetically presents an impressive variety of heroes who deserve a poet to celebrate them. As we saw earlier, Kierkegaard wrote that "the portrayal of the existential is chiefly either realization in life or poetic presentation, *loquere ut videam* [speak so that I may see]" (JP 1 1058). There is no doubt that he spoke as a poet so that many of us see sublime ideals, and read our poet's books, with intense admiration. Perhaps he also *realized* the heroic *in his life* for those with the eyes and hearts to see it. I myself am deeply puzzled about this.

Conclusion

IF WE HAD TO choose between dispassionately understanding Kierkegaard's ideas, on the one hand, and being a little confused about them, but admiring his praise of ideals, and feeling challenged by it, on the other, I have no doubt that we should choose poetic admiration and inspiration. But there is no need to choose. We can understand Kierkegaard's ideas pretty well if we put in the work, and understanding them is crucial if we are going to apply them to our lives. He himself insists that choosing responsibly between or among life-options requires understanding them. This book did not aim primarily at explicating Kierkegaardian doctrine, but instead at helping you to encounter his poetic praise of heroes and ideals for life. But along the way it did explain some doctrine. In this brief conclusion, I will summarize some of his crucial concepts that have been touched on in this book.

In much of his authorship Kierkegaard employs a form of pedagogy that he calls "indirect communication." A major element of this pedagogy is the use of pseudonyms who say things that Kierkegaard himself may not agree with. The resulting uncertainty about his message in many of his books creates difficulties for readers. We cannot trustingly accept what the pseudonyms say as Kierkegaard's own opinion, and we have the task of testing their ideas, their characters, and their lives. In this book we engaged in a fair amount of critical evaluation of several of Kierkegaard's pseudonymous personae. We should also be aware of yet another reason that Kierkegaard's indirect communication can be quite confusing. He thought that human beings tend to delude themselves about important things, and that his generation in Denmark was especially guilty of self-deception. In order to dispel widespread illusions, he resorted to devious tactics by which he aimed to deceive people into the truth. Needless to say, if Kierkegaard is a kind of benevolent deceiver, this fact about him complicates our task as readers. We must become careful, active, and self-reliant, so as not to be taken in by the deceptions that he designed to benefit us.

Whether Kierkegaard is writing directly or indirectly, he is almost always praising something. Praise is ubiquitous in his authorship, and he uses poetry to do it. His poetic celebration of heroes and ideals is meant to inspire us to imitate them. One of his main ideas, *subjectivity*, may be defined as imitating ideals, in one's words, thoughts, deeds, and emotions, as consistently and uncompromisingly as one can. The one who does this lives heroically and poetically. That is, subjectivity is poetry and heroism. One of the most important elements of the idea of subjectivity and the striving that it requires is that human beings are free; and Kierkegaard stresses freedom in many ways. The thought of freedom adds the weight of responsibility to subjectivity. If you are aware of your freedom, you feel passionately that it is up to you to make yourself a copy of the ideal and the heroes who have suffered for the ideal. If we do not own our freedom, but try to avoid thinking about it, Kierkegaard thinks we will be plagued by anxiety, which consists in a repressed, confused, and uneasy awareness of our life-tasks, our freedom, and our responsibility. Worse than anxiety is despair, which consists in losing hope that one can live heroically for ideals that make life worth living. Kierkegaard dedicates a whole book to an examination of anxiety and another book to despair.

Kierkegaard's famous theory of the stages or spheres of human existence corresponds to his ranking of competing ideals and the heroes who represent them. The esthetic sphere is based on the ideal of beauty, and on what we might call the pseudo-ideals of the interesting and pleasure. The character named "A" was our main representative of the esthetic stage of existence. There were also Don Giovanni, who was an immediate and extensive seducer, and Johannes, who was a reflective and intensive seducer. The ethical sphere has many ideals: the good, the noble, the true, fidelity in marriage, and more. Judge William was our symbol of these ideals. Infinite resignation, represented by Johannes de Silentio, was a transitional ideal at the boundary region between ethics and religion. Socrates as ironist, lover, and prophetic truth-seeker symbolizes another transitional ideal at the border between ethics and the religious. The knight of faith, with his double movement, represented the primary Christian ideal. All the ideals, arranged from lowest to highest, map out a path of spiritual growth, and Kierkegaard intends his pseudonymous writings to guide people along the stages on life's way. The relations of the stages have a subtle dialectic that I have begun to describe in this book. One important aspect of their relations is that the higher stages do not demand a complete rejection of the ideals of the lower stages. Instead a higher sphere includes ideals of lower spheres as subordinate elements. We saw, for example, Judge William's explanation of why ethical marriage was more beautiful and therefore more esthetic than anything merely esthetic. Similarly Socrates as an ironic ethicist on the frontier of the religious was the most interesting man who ever lived.

The highest of the ideals according to Kierkegaard is Christ. In order to relate properly to this ideal much work is required to become contemporary with Christ, first by way of poetic imagination, then through existential imitation. Kierkegaard thinks that when one rightly encounters Christ, a decision becomes unavoidable. One option is offense at Christ and at his message about sin, forgiveness, redemption, and the need to participate strenuously in working out one's own salvation in fear and trembling. The other option is to overcome offense by striving to imitate Christ and accepting divine aid in this quest. The strenuous struggle of this quest is according to Kierkegaard the greatest heroism.

Although Kierkegaard is convinced that that highest task is to become a Christian, his generous praise of merely human ideals means that he is a man for all seasons, an author for everyone who senses the need to live for an ideal. As one of his pseudonyms put it, "life has tasks enough also for the person who does not come to faith, and if he loves them honestly, his life will not be wasted, even if it is never comparable to the lives of those who perceived and grasped the highest" (FT 122).

Bibliography

Adler, Alfred. *The Collected Clinical Works of Alfred Adler Volume 1: The Neurotic Character: Fundamentals of a Comparative Individual Psychology and Psychotherapy*. Translated by Cees Koen. Edited by Henry T. Strein. Bellingham, WA: Classical Adlerian Translation Project, 2002.

Aland, Kurt, et al., eds. *The Greek New Testament*. 3rd ed. Stuttgart, Germany: United Bible Societies, 1983.

Brown, Norman O. *Life Against Death: The Psychoanalytical History of Mankind*. Middletown, CT: Wesleyan University Press, 1959.

Evans, C. Stephen. *Kierkegaard and Spirituality: Accountability as the Meaning of Human Existence*. Grand Rapids: Eerdmans, 2019.

Hong, Howard, and Edna Hong. "Historical Introduction." In *The Corsair Affair*, translated by Howard V. Hong and Edna H. Hong, vii–xxxviii. Princeton: Princeton University Press, 2009.

———. "Historical Introduction." In *The Sickness Unto Death*, translated by Howard V. Hong and Edna H. Hong, ix–xxiii. Princeton: Princeton University Press, 1980.

Horace. *Odes and Epodes*. Edited by Paul Shorey and Gordan J. Laing. New York: Benj. H. Sanborn, 1981.

Hume, David. *A Treatise of Human Nature*. London: Penguin, 1986.

Johnson, Samuel. *Samuel Johnson: Selected Essays*. Edited by David Womersley. London: Penguin, 2003.

Jung, C. G. *Jung Contra Freud*. Translated by R. F. C. Hull. New York: Princeton University Press, 1961.

McCombs, Richard. *Art and Praise in Kierkegaard's* Works of Love. Lexington, KY: Lexington, 2023.

———. *The Paradoxical Rationality of Søren Kierkegaard*. Bloomington: Indiana University Press, 2013.

Montaigne, Michel de. "On Experience." In *Michel de Montaigne: The Essays: A Selection*, translated and edited by M. A. Screech, 364–425. London: Penguin, 2004.

———. *Michel de Montaigne: The Essays: A Selection*. Translated and edited by M. A. Screech. London: Penguin, 2004.

Plato. *Platonis Opera*, Tomus I—V. Edited by E. A. Duke et al. New York: Oxford University Press, 1995.

Rousseau, Jean-Jacques. *The Basic Political Writings*. 2nd ed. Translated by Donald A. Cress. Indianapolis: Hackett, 2011.

———. *Emile: or, On Education*. Translated by Allan Bloom. New York: Basic Books, 1979.

Bibliography

Sartre, Jean-Paul. *Existentialism and Human Emotions*. Translated by Hazel E. Barnes. New York: Citadel, 1987.

www.ingramcontent.com/pod-product-compliance
Lightning Source LLC
Chambersburg PA
CBHW031347160426
43196CB00007B/765